Client/Server Computing with ORACLE

Client/Server Computing with ORACLE

Joe Salemi

Ziff-Davis Press
Emeryville, California

Development Editor	Valerie Haynes Perry
Copy Editor	Robin Bornstein
Technical Reviewer	Brian Butler
Project Coordinators	Bill Cassel and Kim Haglund
Proofreader	Cort Day
Cover Illustration	Carrie English
Cover Design	Carrie English
Book Design	Laura Lamar/MAX, San Francisco
Technical Illustration	Cherie Plumlee Computer Graphics and Illustration
Word Processing	Howard Blechman, Cat Haglund, and Allison Levin
Page Layout	Anna L. Marks, Bruce Lundquist, and M. D. Barrera
Indexer	Anne Leach

Ziff-Davis Press books are produced on a Macintosh computer system with the following applications: FrameMaker®, Microsoft® Word, QuarkXPress®, Adobe Illustrator®, Adobe Photoshop®, Adobe Streamline™, MacLink®*Plus*, Aldus® FreeHand™, Collage Plus™.

Ziff-Davis Press
5903 Christie Avenue
Emeryville, CA 94608

ISBN 1-56276-121-8
Manufactured in the United States of America
10 9 8 7 6 5 4 3 2 1

To John K.—Thanks
for all the laughs on
Sunday mornings.
Happy happy, joy joy!

CONTENTS AT A GLANCE

TABLE OF CONTENTS

ACKNOWLEDGMENTS

THIS BOOK WOULD NOT HAVE BEEN POSSIBLE WITHOUT THE HELP, ENCOURagement, and efforts of a lot of folks. I'd like to thank Valerie Haynes Perry, my development editor, for her valuable input on the structure of the book and for making sure we stuck to some type of schedule. I would also like to thank Brian Butler, my technical editor, for ensuring that the book is accurate, and for his many suggestions on topics to add or expand. And, of course, my copy editor, Robin Bornstein, for making sure the book you hold in your hands is written in something that resembles decent English.

J. Stuart Read of Oracle Corp. provided me with a wealth of technical and product information on his company's products, including the early information on and beta copies of ORACLE 7.0. Angela Gunn provided invaluable assistance as my chief researcher on the third-party products included in this book. My thanks to you both; it wouldn't have been possible without you.

I'd also like to thank Bill Cassel, project coordinator, and Cindy Hudson, publisher, of Ziff-Davis Press—Bill for guiding this book through the production process, and Cindy for convincing me that I really should write a second book for ZD Press.

And finally, I'd like to thank Nancy for her unwavering love and encouragement. I couldn't have done this without you.

NOTE: *The original manuscript for this book was printed on recycled paper in order to help the environment—it's the only one we have.*

INTRODUCTION

THE 1990S ARE AN EXCITING TIME TO BE INVOLVED IN THE CLIENT/SERVER database field. More and more organizations are discovering the benefits of C/S computing over the traditional central host systems. And software vendors are constantly releasing new applications and tools that make it easier to set up a C/S system.

ORACLE has been one of the leading relational database management systems for host computers since its initial release in the early 1980s. Late in that decade, Oracle Corp. joined the growing list of database vendors that provide the necessary communications links to turn their host-based databases into C/S databases. ORACLE is now one of the top three C/S database server products in the world.

This book is aimed primarily at two different groups of technical and business managers investigating the C/S architecture for use in their organizations. The first group consists of those who already use ORACLE in a host-based system, and are looking to expand its capabilities to take advantage of the C/S architecture. The second consists of those who have decided the C/S architecture is their organizations' future, and are looking at the systems available.

Chapter 1 gives an overview of current database technology and discusses the elements needed to create a C/S system. Chapter 2 covers the current release of ORACLE, version 6.0, including its features, the platforms it runs on, and how it does C/S communications.

Chapter 3 begins the discussion on creating custom C/S applications with ORACLE's native language, and the application development tools provided in the database package. Chapter 4 continues with coverage of the higher-level application development tools, including those from Oracle Corp. and other third-party software vendors.

Chapters 5 through 9 cover the various third-party software applications designed for use in a C/S system. Chapter 5 discusses the various products available that provide C/S capabilities to your existing database and spreadsheet applications. Chapter 6 covers tools that make it easy to query the data in the database and create reports on it, and Chapter 7 covers products designed to assist managers and executives in analyzing the data as a basis for business decisions.

Chapter 8 presents an overview of some of the other C/S products available today. And Chapter 9 completes the discussions on C/S applications with a look at the highly specialized applications available for particular organizations and industries.

Chapter 10 introduces the next major release of ORACLE; version 7.0, which was slowly being released for various platforms as this book was written. This chapter covers the new features of 7.0, primarily those that make it easier to create a C/S system using ORACLE as the database.

Appendix A provides a chart of all the C/S application products discussed in the book and the platforms they run on. Appendix B is a contact list for the vendors of the products in this book, so you can contact them directly for more information. Finally, a glossary of the terms used in the book is included.

It is my sincerest hope that you find this book helpful in your efforts to use ORACLE as the foundation for a robust C/S system for your organization. Don't look at it as the final word in C/S computing with ORACLE; use it as the starting point for your own investigations into the promising and ever-growing world of client/server database systems.

1

Introducing Client/Server Technology

An Overview of Database Management Systems (DBMSs)

DBMS Architectures

The Client/Server Relationship

Client/Server Platforms

Client/Server Communications

ORACLE and Client/Server Computing

To UNDERSTAND THE DIFFERENT WAYS OF IMPLEMENTING A CLIENT/ server solution using ORACLE, it helps to understand the underlying technologies. A client/server system is composed of three separate technologies working together to provide a way of storing and accessing data. First, there's the software that stores and manipulates the data, called a database or database management system (DBMS). Second, there's the hardware and operating system software on which the DBMS and user applications run. This combination of hardware and software is commonly referred to as the platform. Finally, there's the networking technology that gives the clients the ability to communicate with the server.

This chapter provides an overview of these three technologies and lays the foundation for the specific product discussions throughout the rest of this book. The first section introduces the various types of DBMS models and architectures, with particular attention paid to the relational model (the one on which ORACLE is based). The next section covers in depth the client/ server architecture, including the platforms it runs on and the networking needed to connect those platforms. Finally, we'll take a brief look at how ORACLE fits into the client/server world.

Along the way, we will encounter many terms that are either specific to the world of databases, or used in ways that conflict with their usage elsewhere. I'll define these terms as we go along, and they will also be covered in the glossary at the end of the book.

An Overview of Database Management Systems (DBMSs)

A database system lets us gather together specific pieces or lists of information relevant to us in our jobs or our lives, and store and maintain that information in a central place. The first commercial computers were really nothing more than dedicated database machines used to gather, sort, and report on census information. To this day, one of the most common reasons for purchasing a computer is to run a database system.

A database system consists of two parts: the *database management system* (DBMS), which is the program that organizes and maintains lists of information, and the *database application*, a program that lets us retrieve, view, and update the information stored by the DBMS. It's common for both the DBMS and the database application to reside and execute on the same computer. In many cases the two are combined in a single program; most of the database systems available today are designed this way.

The *client/server* (C/S) architecture increases database processing power by separating the DBMS from the database application; the application runs on one or more user workstations (usually PCs) and communicates with one or more DBMSs running on other computers over a network. While they can be very complex, C/S database systems make the best use of today's powerful computers.

The data stored in a database can be thought of as a population of information. When used this way, *population* describes any group or class of items, objects, or entities that we can define. When we're creating our database, the population we're interested in is the one we need to keep track of, since it becomes the foundation of the database. For example, the population of our database could be the employees of the Acme Anvil Co., the parts in the company's warehouse, or the vendors who supply those parts.

As Figure 1.1 demonstrates, the population of Acme's personnel database is the company's employees, with each record in the database storing the information about a single member of this population. The fields in each record store the important details about that member. In Figure 1.1, a single record contains four fields of information—Last Name, First Name, SSN (for social security number), and Salary—for each member of the population.

Figure 1.1
The elements of a database

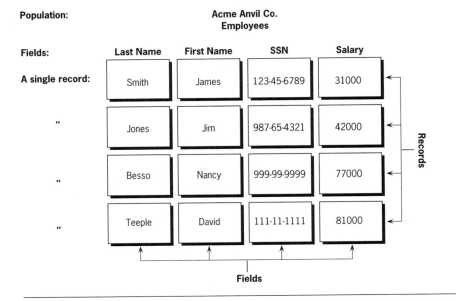

In order to store the population of data on a disk, the DBMS has to provide some type of data definition services to define the records and fields in the database. It also needs an internal mechanism that maintains the data on-disk and knows where each particular element resides.

Of course, we want to do more than just store data; we also need a way to enter or insert data into the database, sort it, retrieve all of it or just portions, and maintain it by adding, updating, or deleting the database records. The DBMS provides some or all of these data manipulation services to the user.

We also need a way to display the data, on a terminal or PC screen, or as a report from a printer. The DBMS can provide these display services as options, or the database application can provide them. If the DBMS doesn't provide these services at all, it's usually referred to as a *database engine*.

Having the data on-disk and retrieving it when we want it isn't any good if we can't trust the accuracy of the data. The DBMS has to provide some type of data integrity services to ensure that the data isn't corrupted through outside means, such as disk crashes or power outages. It also has the more difficult job of protecting the database against unintentional changes by users or applications. These services are particularly important for multiuser databases, where one or more users can be updating the same data at the same time. The DBMS makes sure that only one of the changes actually takes place, and should notify other users when this happens.

A database can store any type of information you want, but to be useful the data has to be stored according to its domain. A *domain* is the category and type of data elements allowed in a particular field—for example, the set of alphabetical (text) characters, integers, or English words. A domain is usually represented as a set, but it can also be restricted to a certain portion of a set, such as positive integers from 1 to 20. Various programming techniques can even use data lookups from another database or file to restrict a field's domain to something as specific as the street names within a particular city. Table 1.1 demonstrates some of the possible domains of the fields in a sample employee database.

Table 1.1	The Domains in the Sample Employee Database

FIELD NAME	DOMAIN
Last Name	[A...Z,a...z,-] (uppercase and lowercase letters and hyphen, or all names containing only these elements)
First Name	[A...Z,a...z] (uppercase and lowercase letters only, or all names containing only these elements)
SSN	[0...9,-] (integers and hyphen, or numbers in the "999-99-9999" format)
Salary	["0.00"..."99,999.99"] (positive decimal numbers between and including 0 and 99,999.99)

The data integrity service of ensuring that the data entered fits the field's domain can be left entirely up to the DBMS, or shared by the DBMS and the user application. This service is the most important job a DBMS can have; the more domain integrity it provides, the better the data integrity of the whole database system.

To pull it all together, we can define a DBMS as an application program that provides the following services:

- data definition for defining and storing a data population

- data maintenance for maintaining records for each item in a population, with fields containing the particulars that describe that item

- data manipulation for letting the user insert, update, delete, and sort data in the database

- data display for optionally providing some method of displaying the data for the user

- data integrity for ensuring the accuracy of the data

DBMS Models

The DBMSs available today can be grouped into four different types, or as they're commonly called, *models*. Each database model describes how the data is presented to the user and programmer for access, and is actually just a conceptual description of how the database works.

A database model also describes the relationship between the different items in the database; for example, in our sample employee database each item of personal information, such as the social security number or salary, is related to the particular employee that the whole record describes. That particular employee's record may also be related to other items in the database, such as the employee's supervisor or department. Note that the relations between the different data items are separate and distinct from the relational model described later on; this is one of those circumstances where the same word has a couple of different meanings, depending on the context.

It's also important to understand that, with one exception, the various models have nothing to do with how the data is actually stored on a disk; this is left to the designers of the DBMS. However, there are circumstances where a model may indirectly place some constraints on how the data is stored if the DBMS is to consist of all the elements or comply with all the rules that make up that particular model.

The four models are the file management system, hierarchical database system, network database system, and relational model. ORACLE follows the relational model, so that's the one I will concentrate on. The descriptions of the other three models are given here primarily as background information.

Historically, the relational model was the first real description of a database model based on computer science theory; the other three models were defined later on to describe databases that had already been in use for several years. The actual evolution of these databases followed the path from file management system to hierarchical database system to network database system to relational model.

File Management System

The *file management system* (FMS) is the easiest data model to understand, and it is the only one that also describes how the data is actually stored on a disk. In the FMS model, each field or data item is stored sequentially on disk in one large file. In order to find a particular item, the DBMS has to search the entire file from the beginning. It can also keep a *pointer* (a logical or physical indicator on the disk) to the last data item retrieved, so that searches for more occurrences of the same data type don't have to begin at the start of the file.

The best example of an FMS is a text document created by a word processing program; each field, or *word*, is stored sequentially in the file. In order to find a particular word, the application has to start at the beginning and check each item until it finds a match. The search can continue from the latest match, or the designer of the database (in this case, the person writing the document) can speed up the search by starting later in the document, assuming that he or she is sure that the item being searched for doesn't appear before this point.

The FMS was the first method used to store data in a computerized database, and its only advantage is its simplicity. Today, about the only DBMS products that are built on this model are the low-end, "flat-file" databases, such Borland's Reflex. Figure 1.2 demonstrates how our sample employee database would look if it were stored in an FMS database.

Figure 1.2
The file management system

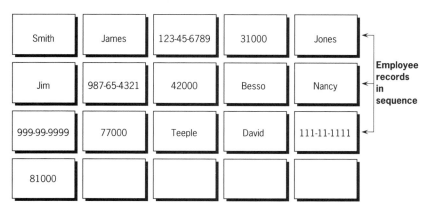

The greatest disadvantage of the FMS is that it doesn't indicate the relationship between the various data items, other than the sequence in which they're stored. There is no quick way to find a particular employee's record, because you have to start from the beginning and examine each and every one.

Also, the only way to sort the data is to read the entire file and rewrite it in the new order. This can easily be solved by using an *index file*, a subset of the data file based on one or more fields, which contains pointers to each record's location in the database. Index files do speed up searches; however, they also add a level of complexity to the database, and they can also get out of sync with the database if you don't constantly update the index as the database changes.

The need for a better way of describing one-to-many relationships among different records, as well as an easier and faster way of conducting searches, led to the development of the next database model.

The Hierarchical Database System

The next logical step up in database models is the *hierarchical database system* (HDS). The data is organized into a tree structure that originates from a root, and each class of data resides at different levels along a particular branch off the root. The data structure at each class level is called a *node;* if there are no further branches to follow, the last node in the series is considered a *leaf*.

As Figure 1.3 demonstrates, the structure of an HDS resembles something that's familiar to just about all of us: the ubiquitous organization chart that's near and dear to the hearts of managers everywhere. In database terms, the tree structure of the HDS defines the "parent-child" and "sibling" relationship between the various items in our database, and clearly shows its advantages over the FMS model for defining one-to-many relationships. It also demonstrates how the hierarchical structure makes the search for data easier and faster: The database simply follows the proper branch without having to search the entire file to find the data it wants. As with the FDS, an index can be used to speed up searches even more, though in the case of an HDS, the index would instead be of a particular class, or level, of data.

In an HDS, there is always a single root node, which is usually "owned" by the system or DBMS. Pointers from the root lead down to the Level 1 nodes (the children of the root node), where the real database begins. The Level 1 nodes represent a particular class of data; in our sample database, that class could be the different departments in the Acme Anvil Co. (Figure 1.4). Each Level 1 node can have one or more Level 2 children, which would represent each department's employees, which are identified by unique identifiers, such as their social security numbers. Each child of the employee identifier class would then contain the information about a particular employee. I've changed the structure of the Level 3 nodes slightly in Figure 1.4, to show the sibling relationship between the different fields, where the path between fields consists of a chain of pointers from one leaf to the next. Any or all of the different levels in an HDS can be diagrammed this way for clarity. Also note that in this model, each child can have pointers to numerous siblings, but only one pointer to the parent, preserving the one-to-many relationship in a single direction.

Figure 1.3

The hierarchical database system

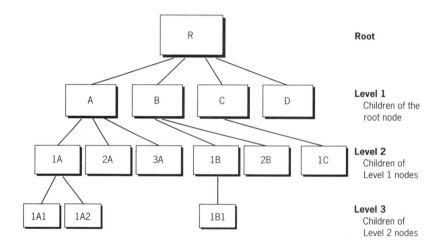

Figure 1.4

The sample employee database in the HDS model

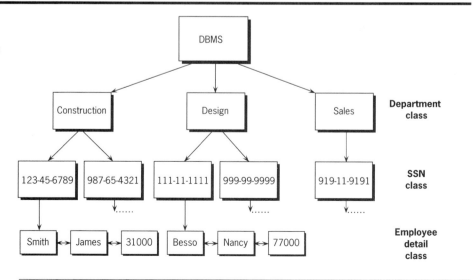

The physical structure of the data on the disk doesn't matter under the HDS model; the DBMS can (and usually does) store the data as a linked list of fields, with pointers that go from parent to child and sibling to sibling, ending in a null or terminal-pointer leaf. It quickly becomes obvious that this design makes it easy to add new fields at any level, as the DBMS only has to change the null terminal pointer to point to the new sibling node (field) in the list. On the other hand, the HDS diagram doesn't quite show which fields make up a particular record. For convenience, we can define a record as a parent and all its children; in our sample database, each employee record would start at the SSN class level and include all the leaves that describe that employee. However, we can also start the record at the Department class level and define a record as all the information about the employees in that department. While this concept gives us a great deal of flexibility, it is not without its problems.

The first problem is that the initial structure of the database is arbitrary and must be defined by the programmer when the database is created. From that point on, the parent-child relationship can't be changed without redesigning the whole structure. In order to make this change, the programmer has to create an entirely new structure, with new parent-child relationships, and copy the data from the original database to the proper locations in the new one.

Instead of restructuring the entire database, the designer could solve this problem by adding another field to each record to store the new information. For example, another leaf could be added to each employee record, identifying the office each is assigned to. This is inefficient, however, as it results in duplicate data and wastes disk space. It also slows a search for all employees assigned to a particular office, as every branch has to be searched all the way to the last leaf in order to find each employee's office identifier.

The biggest disadvantage of the HDS is that it has no easy way to define many-to-many relationships. The most common approach to solving the many-to-many relationship problem is to add secondary parent-child and sibling pointers to the hierarchical structure. This method creates numerous circular relationships; as these relationships become more complex, the database structure eventually evolves into the next model.

The Network Database System

The first written specifications for the network database system were released in 1971 by the Conference on Data System Languages (CODASYL), and to this day DBMSs based on the network database system are usually referred to as CODASYL databases. Note, however, that the name "network" has nothing to do with the physical medium on which the database actually runs; the network database system is a conceptual description of databases where many-to-many (multiple parent-child) relationships exist. To make this model easier to understand, the relationships between the different data items are commonly referred to as *sets* to distinguish them from the strictly parent-child relationships defined by the HDS.

A *network database system* (NDS) relies on either straight-line or cyclical pointers to map the relationships between the different data items. Take the example of Acme's inventory database; in many cases, Acme deals with multiple vendors who sell the same product. Figure 1.5 illustrates a simple (straight-line) form of an inventory NDS, showing the various relationships between parts and suppliers. Using the set-oriented approach, Acme can find out what companies to buy raw iron from by having the DBMS search the Materials set, and then follow the pointers back to the two vendors that supply them. If Acme wanted to know what it buys from Denver Bottled Gas, the DBMS can search the Vendor set for the company name, and then follow the pointers to the two items that it sells. This approach is very flexible, as the DBMS can also treat the combination of a particular vendor and the materials that the vendor sells as a set named "Purchase." In Figure 1.5 this relationship is depicted by the shaded area around Dave's Demolition and the scrap iron and steel this vendor sells.

Figure 1.5

The network database system (simple form)

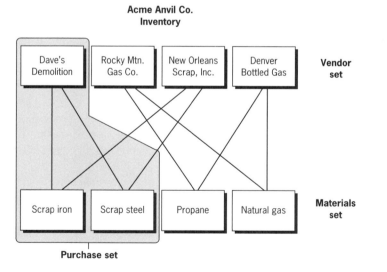

The NDS model can be used to describe even more complex relationships, as Figure 1.6 shows. Suppose Acme wants to know not only the vendors of a particular material, but also how much the company or companies sell it for. Through the addition of a set called Prices, the DBMS can now follow a cyclical path from vendor to material to price. Again, the search can start at any of the defined sets; if Acme decides that it needs more scrap iron, it follows the pointers to the vendor and then follows them to the price the vendor charges (or conversely, to the price and then to the vendor selling it at that price).

Figure 1.6
The network database system (complex form)

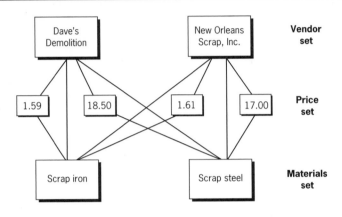

The flexibility of the NDS model in showing many-to-many relationships is its greatest strength, though that flexibility comes at a price. The interrelationships between the different sets can become extremely complex and difficult to map (imagine Figure 1.6 with a hundred vendors, thousands of different materials, and multiple price ranges based on the quantity purchased). Like hierarchical databases, network databases can be very quickly searched, especially through the use of index pointers that lead directly to the first item in a set being searched. The NDS also goes a long way toward eliminating duplicated data.

The NDS model also suffers from the same structural problems as the HDS, however; the initial design of the database is arbitrary, and once it's set up, any changes to the different sets require the programmer to create an entirely new structure. Even so, the NDS does make it simpler to add new data items to the database or change existing ones; the programmer only has to define a new set, and adjust the various pointers to put the new set in the proper relationship with the rest of the data.

The dual problems of duplicated data and an inflexible structure lead to the development of a database model that reduces both problems by making the relationships between the different data items the foundation for how the database is structured. Naturally enough, this model is called the relational model.

The Relational Model

The *relational model* (RM) was first described in a 1969 paper published by Dr. E.F. Codd, an IBM database scientist, who founded the model on the idea of mathematical sets. The RM has been constantly refined since then, most notably by Dr. Codd's paper that laid out the "12 rules" for relational databases (1985), and his book that defines Version 2 (RV/2) of the relational model (1990) through 333 rules that are subsets and expansions on the original 12. Databases based on the RM are so widespread that it's now common to shorten the term "relational DBMS" to "RDBMS".

The RM does away entirely with the concept of parent-child relationships between different data items. Instead, the data is organized in logical mathematical sets, in a tabular (table) structure. The data field becomes a column in a table under the RM, and each record becomes a row in the table. Figure 1.7 demonstrates the Acme inventory database in relational form. Notice that the different sets under the complex NDS model have become different tables, with the particular data items identified by the column names in the first row. All of the vendors are grouped into one table, the materials and prices into other tables. Different relationships between the various tables are then defined through the use of the mathematical set functions, such as JOIN and UNION.

Figure 1.7

The relational model

VENDORS

V#	Vendor_Name	Contact
D1	Dave's Demolition	Dave Johnson
R1	Rocky Mtn. Gas Co.	Becky Campbell
M1	New Orleans Scrap, Inc.	Brad Hayford
D2	Denver Bottled Gas	Jim Jackson

MATERIALS

P#	Part_Description	V#
1001	Scrap iron	D1
5204	Propane	R1
3333	Scrap steel	N1
3333	Scrap steel	D1
5210	Natural gas	D2
5204	Propane	D2
1001	Scrap iron	N1
5210	Natural gas	R1

PRICES

P#	V#	Price	Min_Quan
1001	D1	1.59	10
1001	D1	1.61	1
3333	N1	17.00	1
3333	D1	18.50	1
1001	N1	1.61	1

You'll notice that each table has one or more columns with the same name as that in another table. These common column names are used to relate the different tables. However, the column names don't have to be identical in the RM, as long as the data in the common columns is of the same type and in the same domain.

In order to find a particular material from a particular vendor, the DBMS simply searches the MATERIALS table for the name, finds the vendor number in column V#, and relates it to the similar data in column V# in the VENDORS table to find the vendor's name and contact person. To find the price of the item, the P# and V# columns in the MATERIALS table are related to the same-name columns in the PRICES table. These separate relationships can also be combined, so a user can ask the DBMS to show the vendor, material name, price, and minimum quantity at that price, and the DBMS will do both relations described previously to produce the answer.

Manipulating Tables

The RM has a number of clear advantages over the other models. The most important is its complete flexibility in describing the relationships between the various data items; the only thing the programmer has to do to define the database is to create the tables and decide which columns the tables will use to link each other. From that point on, users can query the database on any of the individual columns in a table, or on the relationships between the different tables. Changing the structure of the database is as simple as adding or deleting columns from a table or creating new tables, and changes don't affect the other tables in any way. New tables can be created from scratch or as projections (subsets) of existing tables, and old tables can be removed at will. Not having to rebuild the entire database structure to make changes also helps preserve data integrity.

The major decision that the designer of a relational database has to make concerns the definitions of the tables. The process of breaking down the data to be stored into subsets for the tables is called *normalization*. The concepts behind normalization are beyond the scope of this book, but in simple terms, the RM defines four levels of normalization, with each level reducing the complexity of the structure from that of the previous one. Each level reduces the amount of duplicated data in the database. As an example of normalization, look at the MATERIALS table in Figure 1.7. You'll notice that even though the P# and Description columns contain some duplicated information, each row of data is unique because the values in the V# column are different for each row. This table can be taken to the next level of normalization by splitting the V# column into multiple columns, as shown in Figure 1.8. This further reduces the amount of space required to store the parts information (though it slightly increases the amount of storage needed for the PRICES table, as the V# column has to be replaced with columns V1 and

V2). It's important to note that these changes in no way affect the data or structure of the VENDORS table.

Figure 1.8
The MATERIALS
table after further
normalization

MATERIALS

P#	Description	V1	V2
1001	Scrap iron	D1	N1
5204	Propane	R1	D2
3333	Scrap steel	D1	N1
5210	Natural gas	R1	D2

In a properly designed RDBMS, the information on the structures that make up the databases is held in a separate set of tables, commonly called the *system tables* or *database dictionary*. This information consists of data elements such as the names of the database's tables, the names of the columns in those tables, and the type of data stored in each column. The DBMS treats these system tables just like any other data table, so the programmer can query them to find out the names of the tables in a database, or the names of the columns in each table.

Preserving Data Integrity

The primary purpose behind the RM is the preservation of data integrity. To be considered truly relational, a DBMS must completely prevent access to the data by any means other than queries handled by the DBMS itself. While the RM (like the HDS and NDS models) says nothing about how the data is stored on the disk, the preservation of data integrity implies that the data must be stored in a format that prevents it from being accessed from outside the DBMS that created it.

The RM also requires that the data be accessed through programs that don't rely on the position of the data in the database. This is in direct contrast with the other database models, where the program has to follow a series of pointers to the data it wants. A program querying a relational database simply asks for the data it wants, and it's up to the DBMS to do the necessary searches and provide the answer. Searches can be sped up by creating an index on one or more columns in a table; however, the DBMS controls and uses the index. The programmer has only to ask the DBMS to create the index and it will be maintained and used automatically from that point on.

The emphasis on data integrity makes the RM ideal for transaction processing systems, and thus for multiuser and C/S databases. In the other database models, changes have to be made directly to the data itself, which can cause conflicts when multiple users are updating the same records. In a relational

DBMS, every change (or group of changes) to the data is treated as a transaction and is done on a temporary copy of the table being changed. Changes don't become permanent until the user or application commits the change to the database itself.

Transactions can also be held in a *transaction log*, which is a disk file that stores a record of all data additions, deletions, and modifications. The transactions are written to the actual database files when the user application commits them, or at certain predefined intervals. Most modern RDBMSs (including ORACLE) use a transaction log. Under either system, the DBMS itself handles conflicting changes to the data and can arbitrate between them. There is a disadvantage to this, in the form of increased system and computational overhead, so a trade-off is made between speedy access to the data and ensuring that the data is accurate.

The Structured Query Language

SQL (structured query language) was designed explicitly as a database language for accessing RDBMSs. The initial version of the language first appeared as SEQUEL in the mid-1970s and was developed by IBM as the standard language for accessing an early relational database that ran on its mainframes. By the late '70s, the name had been shortened to SQL, though there are those who still pronounce it "sequel" out of habit.

The SQL is more properly described as a sublanguage, as it doesn't contain any facilities for screen handling, or user input or output. It's designed for interactive database queries—in which case it is described as *dynamic SQL*—or to be used as part of an application written in one of the procedural languages, where it is described as *embedded SQL*. Its main purpose is to provide a standard method for accessing databases, regardless of the language the rest of the database application is written in.

Since its creation, SQL has gone through a number of revisions. In the early '80s, an attempt was made by the American National Standards Institute (ANSI) to standardize SQL, which led to the release in 1986 of the ANSI SQL Level 1 standard. In 1989 the ANSI SQL Level 2 with Integrity Enhancements standard was released. These standards are sometimes referred to as ANSI-86 SQL and ANSI-89 SQL, respectively. IBM has been at the forefront in expanding SQL, particularly for its DB2 relational mainframe database, to extend the SQL's capabilities. For this reason, it's become common to see the SQL implementations from other DBMS vendors described as "ANSI SQL with DB2 extensions." Attempts are underway to incorporate many of these extensions into the SQL2 specifications due from ANSI within the next few years. However, don't assume that one vendor's SQL implementation can talk to that of another vendor. Every DBMS vendor adds its own extensions to the ANSI SQL standard, and these extensions can make the various SQL versions incompatible with each other. Fortunately, Oracle Corp.

has maintained the same SQL across all the different versions of its RDBMS, so incompatibilities aren't a problem within the Oracle product line.

NOTE. *While the SQL is primarily used and associated with RDBMSs, it's important to note that there is no hard-and-fast rule that says a database that understands SQL has to be relational, or for that matter, that a relational database has to understand SQL. The RM is silent on the subject of languages, other than requiring the language used to access the DBMS to preserve data integrity. There are numerous DBMSs on the market that use SQL yet are only semi-relational, or are based on one of the other database models.*

Until recently, the extra overhead involved in running a relational DBMS kept such databases from being run on all but the largest mainframes and minicomputers. The rise of PCs based on the powerful Intel 80386 and 80486 CPUs has allowed DBMSs that more closely adhere to the RM to move down to microcomputers. This shift has lead to the development of C/S systems, the vast majority of which use an RDBMS on the database server.

DBMS Architectures

The type of computer systems that databases run on can be broken into four broad architectures: centralized, PC, C/S, and distributed. The biggest difference among the four is where the actual data processing takes place.

Centralized Platforms

Mainframes and minicomputers were the original hosts for databases, and to this day they are the primary platforms for large corporate systems. With such a centralized system, everything runs on the host computer, including the DBMS itself, the various applications that access the database, and the communications facilities that send and receive data from the user's terminals. ORACLE was originally developed as a minicomputer RDBMS, and to this day there are many companies using it on a centralized system.

In a centralized system, the users access the database through either locally connected or dial-up (remote) terminals, as shown in Figure 1.9. The terminals are generally "dumb," with little or no processing power of their own, consisting of only a screen, a keyboard, and hardware to communicate with the host. The advent of microprocessors has led to the development of more intelligent terminals in recent years, where the terminal shares some of the responsibility for handling screen drawing and user input. PC-based systems have also gained the ability to communicate with centralized systems through hardware and software combinations that emulate (imitate) the terminal types that are commonly used with a particular host.

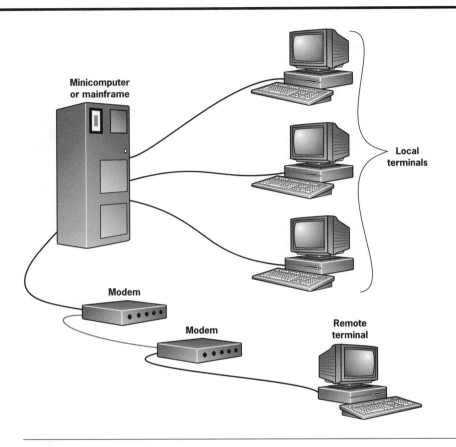

Figure 1.9
A centralized
database system

All the data processing in a centralized system takes place on the host computer, and the DBMS must be running before any database applications can access the database. When the database application starts up, it sends the appropriate screen information "down the wire" to the user's terminal, and takes different actions based on the keystrokes that are sent back from the terminal. The application communicates with the DBMS that's running on the same host through shared memory areas or application task areas that are managed by the host's operating system, and the DBMS handles the task of moving the data to and from the disk storage systems.

The foremost advantages of a centralized system are centralized security and the ability to handle enormous amounts of data on storage devices. Centralized systems also have the advantage of being able to support numerous simultaneous users; it's not uncommon for a database on an IBM mainframe to support over 1,000 users at the same time.

The disadvantages are generally related to the costs of purchasing and maintaining these systems. Large mainframe systems require specialized support facilities, like the fairly common data center with raised floors, water-cooling systems, and very large climate-control systems. Minicomputers are generally more forgiving in their environmental requirements, though some of the larger ones still need at least a climate-control system. A highly trained staff of operators and system programmers is usually necessary to keep the system up and running, which adds considerable personnel costs. Finally, it's not unusual for the hardware for large centralized systems to cost well into the millions of dollars to purchase, with proportional costs for maintenance.

In recent years there has been a trend toward department-size minicomputers, such as Digital's MicroVAX, which don't cost as much to purchase or support, and generally don't require any special environments to run in. These systems are best suited for smaller companies with fewer users, or for database applications that are only of interest to one particular department in a large company. (For example, a minicomputer that runs engineering applications may be of interest only to a design department.) These smaller computers may also be part of a larger network of other minicomputers and mainframes so that all the computers can share common data.

Personal Computer LAN Systems

When a DBMS runs on a PC, the PC acts as both the host computer and the terminal. The separate functions that are done by the DBMS and the database application are combined into one application. Database applications on a PC handle the user input, screen output, and access to the data on the disk. The combination of these different functions into one place gives the DBMS a great deal of power, flexibility, and speed, though usually at the cost of decreased data security and integrity.

PCs originated as standalone systems, where only one person at a time could access the data. However, in recent years many have been connected with each other into *local area networks* (LANs). A LAN extends the reach of a PC and makes it possible for users on different PCs to share access to common data. The data (and usually the user applications) on a LAN reside on the file server, a PC running a special *network operating system* (NOS) such as Microsoft LAN Manager or Novell's NetWare. The file server is responsible for managing the LAN users' shared access to data on its hard disks and other shared resources, such as printers.

While a LAN enables users of PC-based databases to share common data files, it doesn't significantly change how the DBMS works; all the actual data processing is still done on the PC running the database application. The only processing done by the file server is to search its disks for the data file needed by the user, and to send that data file across the network cable to the user's

PC. The data is then processed by the DBMS running on the PC, and any changes to the database require the PC to send the whole data file back to the file server to be stored back on the disk (Figure 1.10).

Figure 1.10

A database on a PC-based LAN

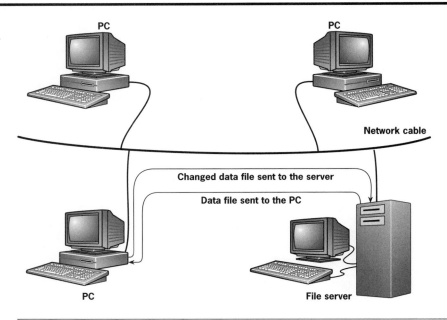

Though multiuser access to shared data is a plus, the biggest disadvantage of a LAN-based DBMS is that regardless of how fast or powerful the file server is, performance is limited by the power of the PC running the actual DBMS. There's also the problem of increased network traffic when multiple users are accessing the database, as the same data files have to be sent from the file server to each and every PC accessing them.

The only enhancement needed by a multiuser DBMS over a single-user one is the ability to handle simultaneous changes to the data by multiple users. This is usually accomplished by some type of locking scheme, where the record or data file that a user is updating or changing is locked to prevent other users from simultaneously accessing or changing it. Most LAN-based DBMSs today are nothing more than multiuser versions of common stand-alone database systems, though the type of locking schemes vary widely and can have significant impact on the performance of a multiuser database.

The majority of PC-based multiuser database systems are capable of handling the same number of users as those based on the smaller, centralized systems, but the problems associated with handling multiple simultaneous

transactions, and the limitations of increased network traffic and processing power of the PCs running the DBMS, are the cause of increasing complexity and performance degradation as the number of users increases. The solution developed for these limitations is the client/server database system.

Client/Server Databases

In its simplest form, a *client/server* (C/S) database splits the database processing between two systems: the client (usually a PC) running the database application, and the database server that runs all or part of the actual DBMS. The LAN file server continues to provide shared resources, such as printers and disk space for applications. The database server can run on the same PC as the file server, or as is more common, on its own computer, which can range in size from a PC to a mainframe. The database application on the client, referred to as the *front-end system,* handles all the screen and user input/output processing. The *back-end system* on the server handles the data processing and disk accesses. For example, a user on the front-end creates a request (query) for data in the database, and the front-end application sends the request across the network to the server. The database server does the actual search and sends back only the data that correctly answers the user's query (Figure 1.11).

Figure 1.11

A client/server system

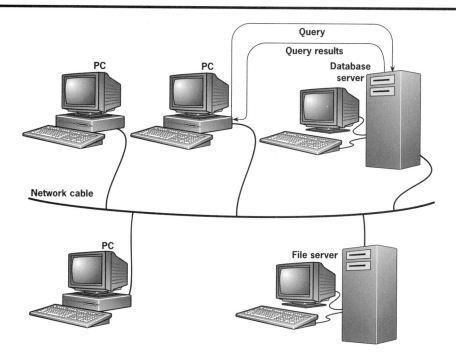

The immediate advantage of a C/S system is obvious: By splitting the processing between two systems, the amount of data traffic on the network cable is significantly reduced. Performance is also improved by running the DBMS on a high-power system, without incurring the expense of upgrading every client system as you would have to if all the processing were done on a local PC.

The biggest disadvantage of the database systems I've described so far is that they require the data to be stored on a single system. This can be a problem for large companies, which may have to support database users scattered over a wide geographical area, or who have the need to share portions of their departmental databases with other departments or a central host. Some way of distributing the data among the various hosts or sites is needed.

Distributed Processing Systems

A simple form of distributed processing has existed for a number of years. In this limited form, data is shared among various host systems via updates sent either through direct connections on the same network, or through remote connections via phones or dedicated data lines. An application runs on one or more of the hosts, extracts the portion of data that's changed during a programmer-defined period, and then transmits the data to either a centralized host or other hosts in the distributed circuit. The other databases are then updated so that all the systems are in sync with each other. This type of distributed processing is usually done between departmental computers or LANs, with the data going to a central host based on a large minicomputer or mainframe after the close of the business day.

While this system is ideal for sharing portions of data among different hosts, it doesn't address the issue of user access to data that's not on the local host. Users have to change their connections to the different hosts to access different databases, and have to remember which database is where. Combining data from databases that exist on different hosts also presents some serious challenges for both users and programmers. Finally, there's the issue of duplicated data; while disk storage systems have declined in price over the years, the costs of providing numerous different disk systems to store the same data can be significant.

The solution to this problem is in an emerging technology of "seamless" data access called *distributed processing*. Under a distributed processing system, a user simply requests data from the local host. The local host then determines that it doesn't have the data and goes into the network to get it from the system that does. It then passes the data back to the user, without the user ever knowing that the data was retrieved from a different system (except, perhaps, for a slight delay in getting the data back). Figure 1.12 diagrams one form of a distributed processing system; the user creates and sends a data query to the local database server. The database server then sends the request for data that it doesn't have over the network to the mainframe (possibly through a gateway or bridge system that joins the two networks together), and gets a response with the results of its query. The local database server then combines those results with the data found on its own disks, and sends everything back to the user.

Figure 1.12
A distributed processing system

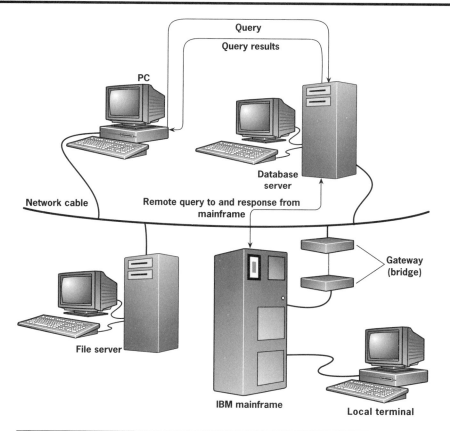

Ideally, this distributed system can also work the other way; terminal users connected directly to the mainframe can have access to data that exists on remote database servers. The design and implementation of distributed processing systems is a very new field. Many pieces aren't in place yet, and existing solutions are not always compatible with each other.

Making sure that the distributed databases are kept in sync also adds complexities to the system. For example, if a user application updates two or more databases at the same time, the DBMSs have to make sure that all the changes to all the databases take place without any errors before permanently saving the changes. If the DMBSs can't make one of the requested changes to one of the databases, the entire transaction has to be rejected, and an error code must be returned to the application. This process is referred to as a *two-phase commit.*

The current version of ORACLE provides some limited distributed processing capabilities, which will be covered in Chapter 2. ORACLE, Version 7.0, which is being released for the various supported platforms during the first few months of 1993, provides even more distributed database features. Chapter 10 provides the latest information available on the new version.

The Client/Server Relationship

Now that we've covered DBMS basics, it's time to examine the specifics of C/S technology. This section will cover the hardware, software, and network technologies used to get a C/S system up and running.

C/S systems can be implemented in a number of ways, mostly determined by the platforms the front and back ends run on, and the degree to which the processing is split between the two.

The Advantages of Client/Server Systems

The primary advantages of a C/S system are the benefits that come from splitting the processing between the client system and the database server. Unlike the traditional PC databases discussed earlier, the speed of the DBMS isn't tied to the speed of the workstation, as the bulk of the database processing is done at the back end. The workstation only has to be capable of running the front-end software, which extends the usable lifetime of older PCs that may not have the horsepower needed to run a complex DBMS.

This also has the effect of reducing the load on the network that connects the workstations; instead of sending the entire database file back and forth on the wire, the network traffic is reduced to queries to and responses from the database server. Some database servers can even store and run procedures and queries on the server itself, reducing the traffic even more. On a large network with many workstations, the reduction in traffic can more than offset the added cost of switching to a C/S system.

Stored procedures and queries can also ensure that different front-end applications use the same code to access the database by providing common, standard routines that the application developers can use. They also make it easier to change queries, as the code only has to be updated in one place, instead of in each different front-end application.

Another benefit of separating the client from the server is workstation independence: Users aren't limited to one type of system or platform. In an

ORACLE-based C/S system, the workstations can be IBM-compatible PCs, Macintoshes, Unix workstations, or any combination of the three. In addition, they can run any of a number of operating systems, such MS-DOS or PC-DOS, Microsoft Windows, IBM's OS/2, or Apple's System 7. A corollary to this is application independence, as the workstations don't all need to use the same DBMS application software. Users can continue to use familiar software to access the database, and developers can design front ends tailored to the workstation on which the software will run, or to the needs of the users running them.

Another major advantage of a C/S system is preservation of data integrity. The DBMS can provide any number of services that protect the data, such as encrypted file storage; real-time backups to tape while the database is being accessed; disk mirroring, where the data is automatically written to a duplicate database on another partition on the same hard disk; and disk duplexing, where the data is automatically written to a duplicate database on a different hard disk. The DBMS also provides some type of transaction processing that keeps track of changes made to the database and corrects problems in case the server crashes.

Transaction processing is a method by which the DBMS keeps a running log of all the modifications made to the database over a period of time. It's primarily used for databases that are constantly being modified, such as an order-processing system, to ensure that the data modifications are properly recorded in the database. The log is used to restore the database (as much as is possible) to a previous error-free state in the event the system crashes while the modifications are being made. Transaction processing capabilities make C/S systems ideal for large multiuser databases, particularly those where multiple modifications to the data can occur at the same time. The DBMS is responsible for handling the locks necessary to prevent multiple changes to the same record or field, and can provide better multiuser access through judicious use of those locks. (For example, you can lock only a record or a field for update instead of locking the whole file.) Contentions and deadlocks between different users modifying the same record are significantly reduced when they're handled by a central DBMS.

The Disadvantages of Client/Server Systems

The major disadvantage of C/S systems is the increased cost of administrative and support personnel to maintain the database server. For a small network (generally under 20 users), the network administrator can usually handle the duties of maintaining the database server, controlling user access to it, and supporting the front-end applications. However, as the number of database server users rises, or as the database itself grows in size, it usually becomes necessary to hire a database administrator just to run the DBMS and support the front ends. Training can also add to the start-up costs, as the DBMS may run on an operating system that the support personnel are unfamiliar with.

There's also an increase in hardware costs. While many of the C/S databases run under the common operating systems (NetWare, OS/2, and Unix), and most of the vendors claim that the DBMS can run on the same hardware side by side with the file server software, it usually makes sense from the performance and data integrity aspects to have the database server running on its own dedicated machine. This usually means purchasing a high-powered platform with a large amount of RAM and hard disk space, as well as additional support equipment such as an *uninterruptible power supply* (UPS) to protect the server from power outages.

The overall cost of the software is usually higher than that of traditional PC-based multiuser DBMSs (though equivalent to or lower than the cost of most minicomputer and mainframe-based central systems). The cost per server for a C/S database that supports unlimited users can range from around $5,000 to tens of thousands of dollars. Add to that the separate cost of the front-end applications or development tools, as well as the personnel costs for training programmers in the new system, and the difference in price over a traditional PC-based DBMS can be substantial.

There's also the issue of complexity. With so many different parts comprising the entire C/S system, Murphy's Law can (and usually does) kick in: The more system pieces, the more things that can go wrong or fail. It's also harder to pinpoint problems when the worst does occur and the system crashes. It can take longer to get everything set up and working in the first place. This is compounded by the general lack of experience and expertise of potential support personnel and programmers, due to the relative newness of the technology. As time goes on and C/S systems become more common, this last problem should abate.

The C/S advantage of application independence also has a down side. Having many different front ends to the database increases the amount of programming support needed as there's more and varied program code to develop and maintain. Making a change to the structure of the database also has a ripple effect throughout the different front ends. It becomes a longer and more complex process to make the necessary changes to the different front-end applications, and it's also harder to keep all of them in sync without seriously disrupting the users' access to the database.

Client/Server Platforms

The *platform* is the hardware and/or software combination on which the C/S DBMS runs. ORACLE runs on all four platforms: PCs, Unix (RISC) workstations and superservers, minicomputers, and mainframes. While the most common platform for C/S computing is a PC, all four have their advantages and disadvantages.

The different hardware systems vary widely in their features and capabilities. However, there are certain common features needed for the operating system software. The *operating system* (OS) is the primary software, which acts as an interface between the hardware and the applications that run on that hardware; applications are usually written to run under a particular OS. Some common examples of OS software are MS-DOS and PC-DOS, OS/2, the many Unix variants, Digital's VMS, and the MVS/XA that runs on IBM mainframes.

The primary OS feature needed for a C/S DBMS is the ability to *multitask,* or run numerous applications concurrently. Multitasking lets the DBMS software properly handle the different user queries and requests without their interfering with each other; this process splits, or *time-slices,* the CPU's processing time between the different tasks or processes. Multitasking operating systems can be preemptive or non-preemptive. In a *preemptive* system, the OS controls the amount of CPU time for each task. In a *non-preemptive* system, the application controls the CPU time, and only gives it up to other tasks when the application's tasks are finished running. Preemptive systems have a natural advantage for C/S databases, as they prevent any one task from dominating the entire system.

The operating system can also be *multiuser* (support simultaneous users doing different tasks), particularly when dumb terminals are used to access the DBMS. A multiuser OS has no particular advantage or disadvantage when used as the platform for a C/S DBMS.

Multithreading is a recent addition to commonly available preemptive multitasking OS software, though the concept dates back to the early '70s. This capability lets an application multitask within itself; for example, a multithreaded single-user DBMS can start a new *thread* (process or task) of execution to do a complex report in the background while the user is doing a query in the foreground. Multithreading has significant implications for designing complex C/S DBMSs, as it gives the application greater control over when a new task is started or stopped. The application can be designed with built-in intelligence to decide which process or task has a higher priority and should be given more CPU time; for example, the DBMS can give slightly higher priority to data modifications over data queries, reducing the performance penalty that the more complex task incurs without significantly affecting the query speed.

There's no one platform that suits every need or is right for every situation. You should first examine your current DBMS systems and project as best you can how much you expect them to grow and how many users you think will simultaneously access them. Then look over the information in this book and choose the platform that can best provide for your present needs and future growth.

Personal Computers

PCs are the most common type of computer available today, but only in recent years have they become an acceptable hardware platform for C/S databases. The advent of high-powered 32-bit 80386- and 80486-based systems, hard disks in the gigabyte (G, or one-billion-byte) range, and stable multitasking operating systems make PCs capable competitors to the RISC workstations and minicomputers that have been the traditional platform for resource-intensive DBMSs.

CPU and RAM Requirements

While a PC based on a 80386 CPU can perform adequately as a database server, the price of 80486-based systems has been steadily dropping over the past year, making the 80486-based PC the platform of choice. For sheer power and future growth potential, the best system to start with is one based on a 50-MHz 80486. Many of the newer PCs come with the CPU on a replaceable card, making it easier to upgrade the system with a faster, 80486 chip, or even a Pentium CPU (Intel's name for its next generation of 80x86 microprocessors) as they become available in 1993.

The next decision is the amount of *RAM* (random access memory) to get for the system. The bare minimum for ORACLE is 8MB, and at least 12MB is recommended for adequate performance. One point to remember when considering a PC for use as a database server: Many of the inexpensive 80486-based systems limit you to 16MB of 32-bit memory. While this amount is fine for high-end workstation use, you definitely want a system that can hold at least 32MB of RAM for a database server. On a NetWare server, for example, 32MB will support 30 to 40 simultaneous users on ORACLE. Even if you don't need that much memory right away, it pays in the long run to have expansion room from the start.

Also be aware that some systems limit the amount of RAM that can be put on the motherboard, and also require additional RAM in the form of proprietary 32-bit add-in cards. Avoid these systems; buy a system that lets you expand to the full 32MB of RAM right on the motherboard. That way you're not locked into buying from one vendor when it comes time to upgrade your servers.

The Hard Disk Subsystem

Probably the most critical component for database performance is the hard disk subsystem, as the bulk of DBMS activities involves reading data from or writing data to them. A hard disk based on the *SCSI* (small computer system interface) standard is your best choice. A single SCSI board can support up to seven attached hard disks, each as large as 1.2GB, giving you an enormous amount of expansion room. While the SCSI standard has its flaws, most hard disk vendors make sure their units are compatible with a wide variety of SCSI cards, so again you're not locked into buying from one vendor.

An interesting alternative is *RAID* (random access independent disk), a type of hard-disk array technology first introduced to the PC market by Compaq for its Systempro line of high-performance servers. This array lets you link a number of smaller hard disks together into what appears to the system to be one large hard disk. It also provides for increased data security, as the hard disks can be set up so they will automatically mirror data among themselves and switch to the backup unit when the primary fails—all without administrator intervention.

Selecting the Bus

Finally, the last decision to make is what type of *bus* (the data connection system for add-on cards) the server should have. The *ISA* (Industry Standard Architecture) bus is based on the original 16-bit bus IBM designed for its PC AT systems. As 32-bit processors became more common, PC vendors saw the need for a 32-bit data bus. Unfortunately, they couldn't agree on a standard. IBM proposed the *MCA* (Micro Channel architecture) standard and implemented it in the company's line of PS/2 computers. However, the otherwise technically excellent MCA bus had two problems to overcome: It isn't backward-compatible with ISA cards, and IBM originally demanded a large licensing fee from other PC vendors. Even though the company has since lowered the fees, the MCA bus hasn't spread much beyond IBM systems.

Compaq and a number of other PC vendors got together and proposed an alternative 32-bit bus standard: *EISA,* for Extended Industry Standard Architecture. The design of the EISA bus lets users continue to use ISA add-on cards while supporting 32-bit EISA cards when needed. The number of PC vendors providing EISA systems has grown over the years, giving users a wide variety of systems to choose from.

Regardless of which bus you decide to use (and the decision should be based on factors besides speed, such as the availability of fast hard disk subsystems and vendor support), go with a 32-bit MCA or EISA system for your database server. Full 32-bit access to the data bus will speed up both hard disk processing and network access speed when 32-bit interface cards are used, eliminating the two biggest bottlenecks a server faces.

Multiprocessor Systems

Multiprocessor (MPU) systems are an emerging technology in the PC world and can have a significant impact on the performance and capabilities of C/S databases. At this time, there are a few MPU systems available that use Intel

80386 or 80486 CPUs; such systems are commonly referred to as *superservers*. We'll discuss which of these systems Oracle supports in Chapter 2.

The Operating System

The first PC-based C/S databases were announced shortly after IBM and Microsoft announced their new protected-mode OS, called OS/2, in early 1987. OS/2 was the first full 16-bit multitasking, multithreaded OS designed expressly for PCs based on 80286 and higher CPUs. Though limited to accessing 16MB of real RAM, version 1.*x* of OS/2 provides superior capabilities over DOS for the resource-intensive database server software; its multitasking capabilities can run multiple services on the same system, including both the LAN software itself and the DBMS. Its multithreading lets applications multitask within themselves, making it easy for software to support numerous users running multiple tasks at the same time. Finally, it has native support for up to 512MB of *virtual memory* (VM), which means that if an application runs out of RAM, the OS can swap portions of unused or idle data to the hard disk to free up working space.

Novell countered the release of OS/2 with a 32-bit version of its *network operating system* (NOS), NetWare 3.0. (NetWare 3.11 is now on the market, and version 4.0 is due sometime in 1993.) NetWare 3.11 can access up to 4G of RAM (though current hardware limitations restrict this to under 100MB of RAM), and it has the ability to run applications on the file server as *NetWare loadable modules* (NLMs). It also provides multitasking and multithreading capabilities but is limited to accessing only the actual RAM present in the system. Early implementations of NetWare 3.*x* had problems running NLMs, but this was quickly fixed; with the release of version 3.11 in 1991, a number of DBMS vendors created NLM versions of their OS/2 or Unix software.

In April of 1992, IBM released its 32-bit version of OS/2, which upped the ante in the database server OS race. OS/2 2.0 increased the amount of real RAM support to 32MB, and it continues support for VM, multitasking, and multithreading. Oracle is currently the only major RDBMS vendor with an OS/2 2.0 version on the market.

Finally, there are versions of Unix that run on 80386- and 80486-based systems, which can be used as the OS for a PC-based C/S database. However, the use of Unix on PCs isn't that common, and it is generally better to go with a hardware platform specifically designed for it if you must run a Unix version of ORACLE.

Which operating system is right for you? ORACLE supports both NetWare and OS/2, so either software platform is acceptable for use on a dedicated database server. (Platforms based on OS/2 can still be used on a NetWare LAN.) There are numerous arguments between supporters of both OS's over the amount of protection these operating systems provide to prevent errant applications from crashing the whole server. NetWare sacrifices protection for speed, and OS/2 sacrifices speed for protection. I think that increased data protection is a primary reason to move to a C/S system in the first place, so at this time my recommendation is to go with an OS/2-based platform. To be fair to Novell, I'll mention that NetWare 4.0 (due for release in mid-1993) is supposed to address the limited protection currently provided, by giving the administrator a choice of sacrificing some speed for increased protection.

In mid-1993, Microsoft will release Microsoft Windows/NT, a 32-bit preemptive, multitasking, and multithreading OS. Windows/NT is being developed to run on multiple hardware systems, including 80386- and 80486-based PCs and a number of RISC workstations. It may become the unifying OS between these disparate systems, and Oracle will port its RDBMS to Windows/NT when the software is released.

NOTE.   *Oracle has an MS-DOS and PC-DOS version of its RDBMS, but I don't recommend using it for anything other than application development purposes. There's a lot of system overhead involved in providing all the services of a C/S DBMS, and DOS, being limited to 640K of RAM, just isn't up to the task.*

RISC Workstations

Workstations based on *RISC* (reduced instruction-set computing) processors are primarily used for scientific or engineering applications, as the RISC CPUs are generally faster and more powerful than Intel's current top of the line, the 80486. A RISC CPU gets its enhanced performance by reducing the amount of microcode in the chip itself; less code means the CPU can perform its internal operations faster. There are numerous RISC chips available today, such as the Sun SPARC, Digital's Alpha, the MIPS line of third-party CPUs, and the Motorola 88000 series. Most RISC chips are proprietary to a single vendor's hardware, but all share similar performance capabilities. Because the usual operating system for a RISC workstation is Unix, in recent years this platform has also come into use as a database server.

The line between a high-powered RISC workstation and a full minicomputer can become very fuzzy; many RISC systems support multiple CPUs and are more properly referred to as superservers. To make things simple, I'm going to refer to workstations as any desktop single-user multitasking system that can also be used as a server, but only through a network connection. Minicomputers and superservers (discussed later in this chapter) are multiuser systems that support both network connections and directly connected terminals.

Most RISC workstations resemble PCs in appearance and operation. They sit on the desktop or alongside the desk in a tower-type case, and they have a keyboard, mouse, and screen (usually a high-resolution color model) directly attached.

RAM and Hard Disk Requirements

A common entry-level workstation comes with 8MB of RAM and anywhere from a 100MB to a 300MB hard disk. This configuration may be fine for a user's system, but as with PCs, more RAM is recommended for a database server. A good working minimum is 16MB of RAM, with support for up to 32MB for later expansion. Of course, a larger hard disk is needed as well, as the Unix OS can easily take up close to 100MB of hard disk space all by itself.

Most of the smaller hard disk subsystems (smaller than 300MB, in the Unix world) are SCSI-based. For larger hard disk subsystems, the vendors use a proprietary hard disk interface for better performance, which can add considerable cost to the workstation.

Having to buy most of your expansion equipment (RAM or hard disk) from the system vendor is the price you pay for getting the extra power of a RISC workstation. RISC systems aren't as widespread as PCs, so a large market for third-party add-ons doesn't yet exist. While an entry-level workstation costs only a little more than a high-powered PC, expanding the system to include server capabilities can in the long run make it cost two to four times as much as an equivalent PC.

Hardware and Software Vendors

There are a number of well-known RISC vendors and systems available today. The systems most commonly used for database servers are the Sun SPARCstation series, IBM RS/6000 series, the workstations put out by the Hewlett-Packard Co. subsidiary Apollo, and Digital's DECStation. Though not as widespread, NeXT Computer's workstations can also be used as database servers.

The increasing interest in C/S computing has led some workstation vendors to create high-powered RISC systems designed explicitly as database servers, which approach the traditional minicomputers in capabilities and power. The best examples of this type of RISC system are Sun's 470 and IBM's RS/6000 POWERServer.

Almost all RISC workstations use a variant of Unix as their operating systems. While at first look this may seem ideal, the truth of the situation is that each vendor's Unix system software is slightly different from another vendor's, so they're not 100 percent compatible with each other. This prevents software vendors from being able to sell one version of their application software that can run on any RISC system, and is the primary reason that RISC workstations haven't become more common on the desktop. Each software vendor has to tailor its application's source code to each Unix variant that the application should support. ORACLE supports over 40 different Unix versions, so these incompatibilities are less of a factor than they would be with other RDBMSs.

The Unix Operating System

Unix is a multitasking operating system, originally developed on a Digital minicomputer at AT&T's Bell Laboratories in New Jersey in the early 1970s, and it is well-suited to multiuser applications. It includes support for virtual memory but generally doesn't support multithreading. The Mach variant used by NeXT is the only multithreaded version to date, though other vendors have promised it in their upcoming OS versions. Most Unix systems are based on one of two variations; Unix System V (the current version of the AT&T original), and Berkeley Unix, a variant developed at the UC Berkeley campus.

Unix has been criticized as a "techie" operating system—hard for most computer users to understand. This criticism is not without merit and should be factored into your decision process. In addition to the extra cost of the RISC workstation platform, it can also be difficult to find support personnel who are familiar with the OS. Some of these objections have been met in recent years through the increased use of a *graphical user interface* (GUI) on Unix systems. Two of the most common Unix GUIs are Sun's Open Look (co-developed with AT&T) and the Open Systems Foundation's Motif (OSF is a consortium of Unix vendors, most notably Digital, HP/Apollo, and IBM). These GUIs add a degree of user friendliness to Unix and make it somewhat easier to use and support. Sun includes Open Look in its Solaris operating system, and IBM and Digital include Motif in their Unix variants (AIX and ULTRIX, respectively).

Minicomputers and Superservers

Minicomputers and mainframes are the traditional workhorses when it comes to database applications, and minicomputers are generally optimized for multiuser applications. In recent years, various methods of connecting a minicomputer to a PC-based LAN have been developed, and it's now possible to use a minicomputer as both a file server and a database server.

Many businesses already have one or more minicomputers. A C/S DBMS can enhance the minicomputer's capabilities by extending data access to the many PCs and LANs in the company. A C/S system also reduces the workload on the minicomputer by moving part of the processing to the front-end system, which lets the minicomputer support more users without expanded or enhanced hardware. The initial costs involved in purchasing and setting up a C/S DBMS can often be more than offset by the savings of not having to purchase additional hardware.

Minicomputers are usually based on proprietary CPUs and expansion equipment, and they range in size from small towercases to boxes that resemble overgrown refrigerators. Superservers are a type of minicomputer that uses standard Intel or RISC CPUs, and they usually run a Unix variant. A minicomputer usually has a number of serial ports for connecting dumb terminals, and a network card is a common option. They support much more RAM than is supported by PCs or workstations, and are thus better suited for applications that allow hundreds of users simultaneous access.

The high-end minicomputers also support multiple CPUs in the same box, adding both processing power and system redundancy in case of failure.

Minicomputers also support high-speed hard disk subsystems that can range into the hundreds and thousands of gigabytes, making them well suited for company-size databases. These subsystems usually support fault tolerance as an option, through disk mirroring and/or duplexing, providing more data redundancy and integrity.

Most minicomputers can be *clustered*, meaning two or more machines are linked together through high-speed connections, and all the machines in the cluster share the same hard disks. Clustering lets users expand the capabilities of the computer (such as the number of users supported) without forcing you to purchase more hard disks or move data between different machines.

Minicomputers and superservers suffer from the same problem as RISC workstations: the general lack of third-party expansion products. In most cases, purchasing a minicomputer locks you into buying all future equipment from the same vendor, at proportionally higher costs.

Some of the more common minicomputers are those from Digital and HP. Digital's line ranges from the tower-size MicroVAX to the refrigerator-size VAX 6000. HP's HP3000 series comes in both proprietary CPU and RISC CPU models. Common examples of a superserver are the computers from Sequent and Teradata.

Just about all minicomputers use a proprietary OS, with Unix as an option. Digital's systems are based on VAX/VMS, and HP has both the older MPE OS, along with its new MPE/XL OS designed for RISC-based systems. Superservers usually run Unix.

Digital's ULTRIX also runs on the entire VAX line. HP's version of Unix is HP-UX, a variation of AT&T's Unix. The Teradata machines run either Unix or their own customized version of MS-DOS. Running Unix on a minicomputer has the advantage of giving you a wider choice of applications software and DBMSs, and in general a larger pool of support personnel to choose from.

There are also versions of NetWare available for VMS and Unix systems, as well as LAN Manager/X for Unix systems. Both let you use a minicomputer as a file server on a PC-based LAN through a familiar NOS interface. However, the degree of integration between the LAN software and the native minicomputer system varies, and the LAN NOS may run just as an application on the minicomputer host, without giving you access to other applications running on the same machine. Before you decide to use a minicomputer as a LAN server, make sure that the particular minicomputer's OS supports access to the applications you need through the NOS. In general, it's better (and cheaper) to use the minicomputer's native OS instead of increasing the system's complexity by tacking a separate NOS on top.

Mainframes

The mainframe is the most powerful general-purpose computer available; it supports multiple high-speed processors, enormous amounts of hard disk space, and hundreds to thousands of simultaneous users. Mainframes offer the most security of any available systems, in terms of both data security and hardware redundancy. Mainframes are also the most expensive computers available, in terms of hardware, software, support environments, and personnel. Unlike the smaller computer systems, a mainframe requires a controlled environment, including constant temperature control, raised floors, and even special cooling equipment (the larger mainframes are still water-cooled). Because of this, mainframes are usually found in company-owned data centers, which can be located in either a separate section of a company's office building or a completely separate building.

Today's mainframes can support hundreds and even thousands of users accessing multiple applications through terminals or network connections. While still used as the primary system for central database applications in many large companies (IBM recently started calling mainframes the "data warehouses" for large businesses), the rapid spread of PCs and workstations has led to a slow evolution in the role of the mainframe as host for C/S DBMSs.

It was in the mainframe world that the term *mission-critical* was first used, referring to database applications that are so critical to a business's operations that the business could collapse if the data wasn't available. For this reason, the mainframe is still looked upon as the most important system for central data storage for large corporations. Even with moves toward downsizing corporate databases to minicomputers and PC-based LANs, mainframes will be around for years to come, fulfilling their role as data warehouses.

Hardware Subsystems

Unlike most other computers, a mainframe is not contained in a single box. It usually consists of a number of different subsystems that handle different tasks, all linked together through high-speed copper wire, fiber-optic cables, or both. Typical subsystems include CPUs, RAM modules, communications systems, hard disks, and tape drives.

The computer is accessed through terminals or PCs with terminal emulators, which are connected to terminal controllers (specialized subsystems that handle the terminal's communications network connections) that are then connected to the mainframe. Dial-in access is accomplished through a *front-end processor* (FEP), a hardware subsystem not to be confused with the front-end applications used to access a C/S database. This processor handles the communications between the remote terminals and the central host.

Network connections are also accomplished through add-in controllers that go into the FEP.

The mainframe's processing power and speed comes from proprietary multiple CPUs, high-speed hard disks, and high-speed communications paths between all the different elements that make up the system. Fault-tolerant hard disk subsystems, along with redundant processing systems and data paths, are also a typical feature. Mainframes generally contain more than 256MB of RAM; the top-end machines can support gigabytes of RAM. The hard disk subsystem sizes are measured in the hundreds of gigabytes, and it's not uncommon for a mainframe to have hard disks that hold more than a terabyte (1 trillion bytes) of data.

IBM versus Digital

The most common mainframes are those put out by IBM; they range in size from the 4381's, which are not much larger than some of the bigger minicomputers and support only a few hundred users, to the room-filling 390 series, which can support thousands of users. There are also IBM-compatible mainframes available, such as those from Ahmdal and Fujitsu Computer Products of America.

IBM mainframes were the host to the original developments in multitasking and multiuser OS software, and today run the most sophisticated OSs available. Mainframe OSs are very modularized, with different subsystems handling which task runs on which CPU, communications with the hard disk and tape storage subsystems, and user interactions with the computer.

IBM's mainframes run one of two proprietary multitasking, multiuser OSs: VM (usually on the low to midrange systems), and various versions of MVS (such as MVS/XA and MVS/ESA) on the midrange and high-end systems. IBM also provides a version of AIX that lets users run Unix applications on the mainframe. The underlying IBM OS software is only a part of the whole. All it provides is the system services. Other system-level software from IBM or third-party vendors provides the interface between the users and the applications on the mainframe, and specialized security software governs user access and data security.

Digital's top-of-the-line VAX 9000 series also qualifies as a mainframe based on its size and the number of users supported, and it has most of the same hardware support requirements as other mainframe systems.

Digital's mainframes primarily run on the same VAX/VMS OS as its minicomputers and can be clustered with the minicomputers as a company's data processing needs grow. Digital's Unix-variant ULTRIX is also an option on the 9000 series.

IBM and Digital mainframes have existed long enough for the development of a stable third-party hardware industry that provides "plug-compatible" disk and tape drives, FEPs, terminal controllers, and terminals that can be added to the system without the need for special adapters. While most of the third-party hardware is cheaper than equivalent parts from IBM and Digital, the overall cost of mainframe equipment is usually measured in the hundreds of thousands to millions of dollars.

The Downsizing Trend

The interrelationships between the various system-level software applications and user applications add an enormous cost to the mainframe system in terms of support personnel. It's not uncommon for a corporation with a mainframe to have an entire *information systems* (IS) or sometimes a *management information services* (MIS) department consisting of system programmers, communications network specialists, and system operators to keep the whole system up and running. Program analysts and applications programmers are also necessary to create the applications for the ultimate end users of the mainframe, since most mainframe applications are custom-written.

These large personnel and maintenance costs have led to the concept of and trend toward downsizing mainframe systems to minicomputers and PCs, as the smaller systems have increased in power and features. These C/S systems are approaching the power and capabilities of many mainframe applications and use more "off-the-shelf" software that doesn't require such large support staffs.

However, the smaller systems cannot yet completely replace mainframes as the systems of choice for large, corporation-wide databases. Because of this, the mainframe and Digital VAX versions of ORACLE are still in widespread use and will remain so for the foreseeable future.

The trend today is toward integrating existing mainframes into new corporation-wide C/S systems rather than toward installing new mainframes, and it's in this light that I'll discuss the mainframe version of ORACLE later in this book.

Client/Server Communications

A C/S database system depends on the processing being split between an intelligent front-end system and the database server. The obvious implication is that some method must exist for these two parts of the system to communicate with each other. The topic of computer networks is beyond the scope of this book. You can find detailed information about them in other Ziff-Davis Press books, particularly the second edition of the *PC Magazine Guide to Connectivity* and the *PC Magazine Guide to Linking LANs*, both by Frank J. Derfler, Jr. I'll just cover some of the basic concepts necessary for understanding how clients and servers communicate with each other.

The client systems communicate with the server through a network consisting of a combination of hardware and software. The hardware consists of a *network interface card* (NIC) that's added to the PC, workstation, and server, and connects the PC to the network's wiring. (In some cases, the NIC is built right into the system.)

A LAN has networked PCs, workstations, and servers that are all in the same building. When a LAN extends across buildings (on the same campus or across the country, for example), the entire network is referred to as a *wide area network,* or WAN.

LAN Topologies

There are three LAN topologies in common use today: Ethernet, Token-Ring, and ARCnet. Unless some type of bridging system is used, all the PCs and servers on the network must have NICs that support the same topology. An Ethernet system commonly runs at 10 megabits per second (Mbps), and uses either coaxial cable in a *bus* (daisy-chain) configuration, or *twisted-pair* (TP) cable in a hub-and-star configuration from one or more central concentrators (Figures 1.13 and 1.14, respectively).

Figure 1.13

An Ethernet-bus network

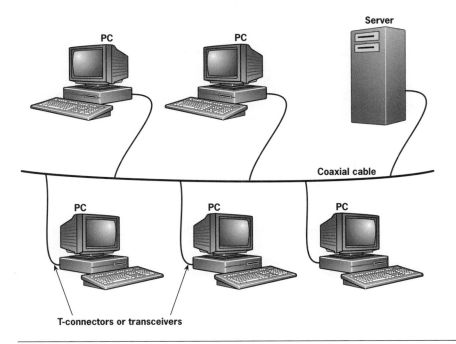

Figure 1.14
A twisted-pair
Ethernet network

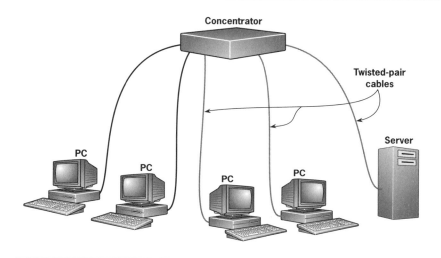

Token-Ring is a token-passing network that uses twisted-pair wiring in a ring configuration, and runs at 4 or 16 Mbps (Figure 1.15). Note that most Token-Ring networks actually resemble star-and-hub Ethernet networks, as the ring really exists in the central wiring closet between the various *multistation access units* (MAUs).

ARCnet is a 2-Mbps Token-Ring network, and it uses a series of active and passive hubs connected with coaxial cable (Figure 1.16). Passive hubs connect to the PCs, and active hubs connect the passive hubs to other passive hubs and PCs. A 20-Mbps version of ARCnet has been announced but is not yet available.

The Hardware: Cables, Modems, and Drivers

Due to the speed limitations of copper-based cable, high-speed fiber-optic (light-based) cabling schemes have come into increasing use. Fiber-optic cabling is generally more expensive to install and support than copper cable (though it's much more resistant to electrical interference), so fiber optics is most commonly used for connecting LANs on different floors to a building-wide backbone, or as a high-speed link between different LANs across a campus. Widely scattered WANs can be linked through standard telephone lines via modems, though current technology limits these links to 38,400 bits per second. Higher-speed (and higher-cost) WANs can be linked with special modems through data-grade T-1 (1.54-Mbps) phone lines provided by all the

Figure 1.15

A Token-Ring network

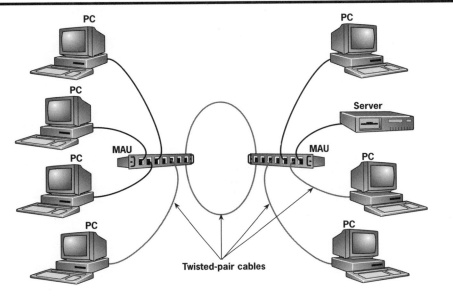

Figure 1.16

An ARCnet network

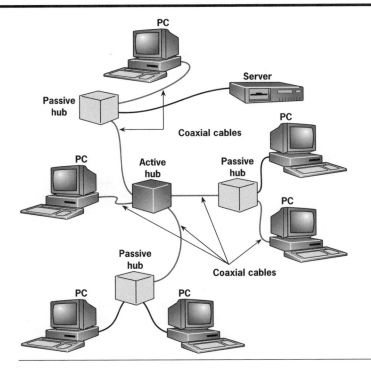

major telephone companies. Modems are also used for individual remote PCs to dial in and connect to the LAN in order to share data and services.

Once the PCs are connected to the network cabling, installed software drivers tell the PC how to communicate on the cable through the NIC. Other drivers allow the PC's user and applications to access data and files on the LAN's file server, send print jobs to shared printers on the server, or communicate with the database server.

Network Protocols

A *protocol* is simply a standard method by which two computer systems communicate across a network. Many proprietary network protocols exist today, but only a few concern us when designing a C/S database system.

NetWare LANs use Novell's IPX (Internet Packet Exchange) protocol to provide communications between the workstations and the server or servers. Microsoft's LAN Manager and IBM's LAN Server use variations of the NetBIOS protocol, and Digital-based LANs use the DECNet LAT protocol. IBM mainframes primarily use SNA to communicate to terminals and LAN Gateways, and IBM's LANs also support the DLC protocol for direct communications between the LAN PCs and the mainframe FEPs.

The most common cross-platform protocol is TCP/IP. Originally developed as the Unix networking protocol, TCP/IP is now available for just about every platform and OS, and is widely used for linking PCs, workstations, minicomputers, and sometimes mainframes.

While sufficient enough for basic LAN communications, these protocols generally don't provide enough data space for C/S applications, so a second protocol layer is required. ORACLE uses its own protocol, called SQL*NET, which will be discussed in more detail in the next chapter.

ORACLE and Client/Server Computing

ORACLE started its life on minicomputers, and it is still used by many sites as the primary RDBMS on a centralized system. However, the development of SQL*NET in the late 1980s gave ORACLE the ability to run as a database server in C/S systems. It's now the second-most-popular C/S DBMS for PC-based systems, and the most popular RDBMS overall.

The next chapter will cover ORACLE 6.0, the current widely available version, and will focus on its DBMS features, the platforms it runs on, and its C/S capabilities. ORACLE 7.0 is scheduled for release in early 1993 and will extend and improve on the current version's RDBMS and C/S capabilities; I'll be detailing the improvements in the new version in Chapter 10.

2

Oracle, Version 6.0

Evaluating the Current Version

Supported Platforms

Networking with ORACLE

O RACLE CORP. HAS THE DISTINCTION OF BEING THE FIRST COMPANY TO create and sell a commercial RDBMS that used SQL, preceding IBM's release of its own SQL-based RDBMS by about two years. The early versions were developed on Digital VAX/VMS systems, and VMS remains Oracle's primary platform; all new versions of ORACLE come out for the VMS operating system first.

Corporations looking to create a complete client/server system that can include everything from PC LANs to mainframes can use ORACLE as the common RDBMS for all of their platforms, which reduces the need (and cost) to train programmers, developers, and support personnel how to use multiple database systems. In addition, ORACLE users can draw on a large pool of applications developers already familiar with the software when hiring new personnel.

Evaluating the Current Version

ORACLE, version 6.0, is the current widespread release; different platform versions may have a sub-version number, such as 6.0.1, that represents a release with a minor bug fix for that platform. Version 7.0 (which I'll be covering in Chapter 10) was in limited release for VAX/VMS systems at the end of 1992; it should be available for all supported platforms by the end of 1993, according to Oracle's development and distribution schedule.

Like most high-end computer software packages, ORACLE is available from three sources:

- Direct from Oracle

- From third-party hardware vendors that have reseller agreements with Oracle

- From independent ORACLE application developers and *value-added resellers* (VARs)

Features and Capabilities

ORACLE's most powerful features are its portability and scalability. Versions are available for virtually every major hardware and software platform in existence, including PCs, Macintoshes, mainframes, and most Unix variants. Application code written for one platform can easily be ported to another one, because of Oracle's SQL pre-compiler (which will be covered in Chapter 3). PC-based versions of Oracle are available for MS-DOS and PC-DOS, OS/2 1.3 and 2.0, and as an NLM for NetWare 3.11. ORACLE versions are also available for over 40 different Unix variants.

ORACLE provides the strongest distributed processing support of any of the C/S databases available at this time. The key to this database distribution is Oracle's SQL*NET communication protocol, which I'll be discussing in further detail at the end of this chapter.

Version 6.0 supports distributed queries only through database links; data on the remote server can't be modified through the link. Distributed queries can be slow and are not widely used. However, different versions of SQL* NET can be simultaneously run on the client workstation (if there's enough available memory), allowing the client to connect directly to different Oracle databases running different protocols at the same time. When done this way, each connection supports the full capabilities of the user's application, so the user can view and modify data on any of the connected databases. This method also doesn't suffer from the slow performance of distributed queries.

Oracle databases can be split among different hard disks or volumes, giving them, for example, a maximum size of 2GB under OS/2 or 4GB for the NLM version. Database sizes on other platforms are limited only by the operating system and hard disk space available. Oracle's ability to connect to other Oracle servers also gives the *database administrator* (DBA) the ability to create "virtual databases" with limits that are many times larger than those imposed by a single server. Be aware, though, that server performance can suffer when you use a virtual database.

ORACLE also uses two text files to control system configuration and performance parameters: INIT.ORA and CONFIG.ORA. Default versions of these files are installed on the disk when you install the package, and you can edit them with any text editor appropriate for your system. Appendix E of the *Database Administrator's Guide* contains the details on INIT.ORA, and Appendix F covers CONFIG.ORA.

Oracle also has a number of products that let ORACLE users access data on non-Oracle databases. Both SQL*Connect to DB2 and SQL*Connect to SQL/DS connect ORACLE databases to IBM's mainframe-based RDBMSs, and SQL*Connect to RMS links Oracle to Digital's VAX/VMS-based RMS database. By using various versions of the ORACLE RDBMS and one of the SQL*Connect gateways, an *MIS* (management information systems) department can create the most complete distributed database system available today.

The manuals that come with the ORACLE database server are also very helpful, with complete and detailed explanations of the RM, and all the various functions and capabilities of the RDBMS. As with any computer manual, there are some errors; however, the documentation is still a valuable resource for properly setting up, configuring, and tuning your ORACLE server. I strongly advise you to read through them at least once, and keep them handy for future reference.

ORACLE's price varies, depending on the platform and sometimes the number of users; it can range from $3,999 for the eight-user OS/2 2.0 version to $298,000 for the full IBM-mainframe MVS version. The best source for price information is your Oracle sales representative or VAR.

Databases and Tables

ORACLE's system tables are called the *data dictionary.* Information on users, user rights (privileges), database components (such as tables), views and indexes, default values, data constraints, and other database functions is stored here. The data dictionary stores its information in columns and rows, and the DBA can query it just like any other ORACLE database. A full reference to the information stored in the data dictionary can be found in Appendix G of the ORACLE Server *Database Administrator's Guide.*

All platform-specific versions of version 6.0 share the same datatypes, as shown in Table 2.1. Many of these datatypes are enhanced in version 7.0; see Chapter 10 for details. Table 2.2 details the different maximum sizes for version 6.0's tables and databases.

Table 2.1 | **Datatypes for ORACLE, Version 6.0**

Datatype	Description
CHAR and VARCHAR	Any characters or alphanumeric data, in ASCII or EBCDIC format, depending on the platform. CHAR and VARCHAR are equivalent in version 6.0, with a maximum size of 255 characters.
DATE	Dates and times. Dates can range from January 1, 4712 BC to December 31, 4712 AD. Time is stored in a 24-hour format, as HH:MM:SS (hours:minutes:seconds).
LONG	Variable-length character or alphanumeric strings, up to 65,535 characters. Each table in a database can have only one LONG column.
LONG RAW	Similar to LONG, except that it can also store binary data. LONG RAW data is not converted to characters when transmitted to a workstation or another database server.
NULL	The lack of value in a column, or missing data. NULL is not so much a datatype as it is the absence of data.
NUMBER	Any fixed or floating-point digits. Floating-point numbers are stored with up to 38 digits of precision; the maximum value is 9.99×10^{124}, or a 1 followed by 125 zeros.
RAW	Similar to CHAR and VARCHAR, except that it can also store binary data. RAW data is not converted to characters when it is transmitted to a workstation or another database server.

Table 2.1 | **Datatypes for ORACLE, Version 6.0 (Continued)**

Datatype	Description
ROWI	A pseudo-datatype that corresponds to the address of a row of data in the database. ORACLE automatically assigns a value for ROWID to every row of data. Users can access but not modify the value stored here.

Table 2.2 | **Limits of ORACLE, Version 6.0**

Database or Table Specification	Limit
Database size	OS/2, 2GB; NLM, 4GB; other platforms, depends on hard disk space
Column size	65,535 characters
Row size	65,535 characters
Number of columns in a row	254
Number of rows per table	Limited by hard disk space
Number of rows per database	Limited by hard disk space
Number of tables per database	Limited by hard disk space
Number of views per database	Limited by hard disk space
Number of tables per view	No limit, with up to 254 columns per view

ORACLE's SQL is compatible with the ANSI SQL Level 2 standard. Though version 6 includes some of the keywords specified by the Integrity Addendum, the DBMS doesn't enforce them; they're present only for DB2 syntax compatibility. It's still up to the application programmer to check and enforce *relational integrity* (RI) and *data integrity* (DI). The server-based integrity features will be a part of version 7.0. ORACLE also supports its own extensions to SQL, called *Procedural Language/SQL*, or PL/SQL for short. I'll be exploring these native languages further in Chapter 3.

Administration

The only front end provided with ORACLE is SQL*DBA, a character-mode command-line interface that's used to administrate and query databases. In addition to executing directly entered SQL statements, SQL*DBA can execute a series of SQL and PL/SQL statements stored in a text file.

SQL*DBA has some built-in administration functions, including a real-time database monitor that lets the administrator examine the current and historical database access, existing database locks, current user activity, and server performance statistics (as shown in Figure 2.1). It comes in the appropriate version for the database server operating system; in addition, the DOS and OS/2 versions of SQL*DBA are included in the OS/2 server package, and NLM and DOS versions are included in the NetWare 3.11 server package.

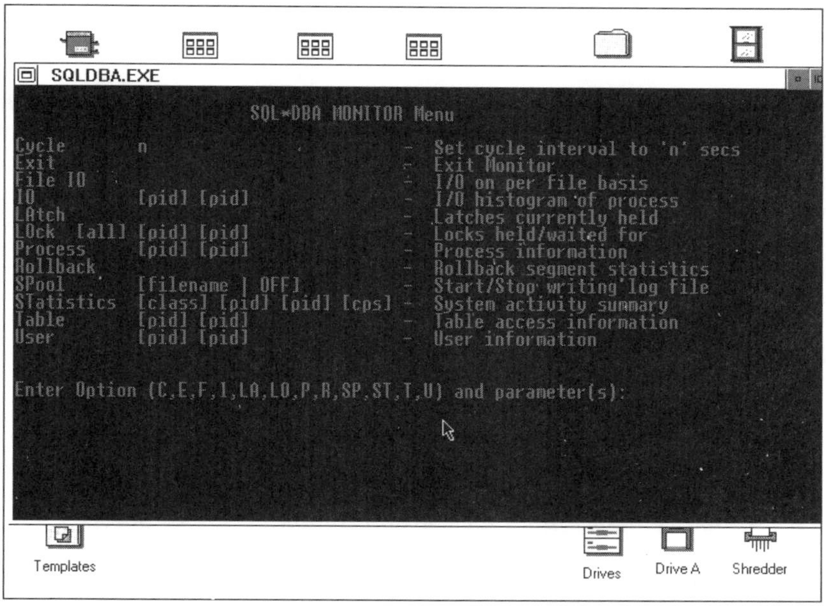

Figure 2.1
ORACLE's SQL*DBA command-line interface, which also acts as a comprehensive system monitor

SQL*DBA can be run either on the server or from a workstation communicating with the server via SQL*NET. Any platform-specific version of SQL*DBA can be used to administrate any ORACLE database, as long as the proper version of SQL*NET is loaded.

Disadvantages

ORACLE, version 6.0, is almost three years old, and it unfortunately no longer leads the market in technical excellence. It lacks features commonly found in other SQL C/S database servers—stored procedures, triggers, declarative referential integrity, and cost-based optimization. It's also a re-source hog: For example, every user accessing an OS/2- or NetWare-based server requires at least an additional 250K of RAM on the server, as each user connection starts a completely new server process. When the overhead of the NOS and the ORACLE software itself is added, a 16MB server can effectively support only between 16 and 20 users without slowing to a crawl. Because of this, the OS/2 version is limited to a maximum of 48 users, and the NLM version to a maximum of 96 users. On minicomputers and mainframes, the number of users per ORACLE database depends on the capabilities of the hardware and software platforms.

Better use and management of resources is one of the primary new fea-tures in version 7.0. This version of ORACLE will be able to support at least 2 to 3 times as many users as version 6.0 on the same platform.

Ironically, another of ORACLE's greatest weaknesses is having so many different platforms to support. New versions are always released for the VAX/VMS platform first, and the expanding C/S market means that Oracle will concentrate on porting version 7.0 to PC-based and Unix platforms next. It may be some time before version 7.0 is ported to mainframe operating sys-tems; in the case of version 6.0, the time lag between the initial VAX/VMS release and the release of the mainframe versions was over a year.

Supported Platforms

Oracle has committed itself to supporting a wide variety of hardware and soft-ware platforms, which has made ORACLE the top-selling RDBMS in the world today. The company was one of the first to produce a DOS-based RDBMS. Oracle continued its string of firsts, as it was the first vendor to re-lease a full 32-bit OS/2 2.0 version of its DBMS, and one of the first to release a NetWare 3.1 NLM version.

Hardware

Version 6.0 runs on every hardware platform size, including PCs, Digital's VAX systems, IBM mainframes, and most RISC workstations and superserv-ers. As mentioned previously, ORACLE demands a lot of memory resources from the server; this is particularly true with PCs. The OS/2 2.0 version re-quires at least 12MB of RAM, though a minimum of 32MB is needed to sup-port the maximum number of users. The software itself takes up less than 10MB of hard disk space.

The NLM version requires at least 16MB of RAM; in this case, a mini-mum of 96MB is needed to support the maximum number of users without causing severe performance degradations. The requirements of other hardware platforms vary, depending on the operating system overhead and the capabilities of the hardware itself.

Versions of ORACLE are also available for a number of *multiprocessor* (MP) systems, such as those available from nCUBE and Sequent Computer Systems, and they take full advantage of MP capabilities. Oracle was the first RDBMS vendor to provide a version specifically designed for parallel-processing systems, and this company's implementation is considered the best available by a number of database experts.

Operating Systems

For PCs, ORACLE is available for MS-DOS and PC-DOS, OS/2 1.3 and 2.0, and NetWare 3.11. However, the DOS version is restricted in its capabilities because of the operating system's limitations (primarily its RAM limitation and its single-user-only capability), and I don't recommend using it except as a single-user application development platform. Versions are also available for PC-based versions of Unix, such as SCO's XENIX, as well as over 30 other versions of Unix, such as AT&T System V, IBM's AIX, Digital's ULTRIX, and Sun's SunOS and Solaris.

VAX/VMS is ORACLE's native platform, and versions are available for all types of Digital minicomputers and mainframes. Versions are also available for IBM and IBM-compatible mainframes that run the VM or MVS operating system. Oracle's two mainframe gateways can run on the same system, and they provide ORACLE users with transparent access to IBM's mainframe-based SQL/DS and DB2 databases. Client systems simply send their SQL commands to the ORACLE database, which passes the data requests through SQL*Connect for processing.

Networking with ORACLE

There are many copies of ORACLE still in use as centralized databases running on a minicomputer or mainframe. Users access the database through terminals, and all of the processing takes place on the host computer.

However, C/S computing symbolizes the present and future of advanced database processing capabilities, and Oracle is well represented in this field. It was one of the earliest supporters of the C/S technology, and Oracle has continued to enhance its products' support for this technology.

SQL*NET

The key to ORACLE's C/S and distributed processing capabilities is the SQL*NET communication protocol. Multiple versions of SQL*NET can be run at the same time on an ORACLE server, which lets the server handle links to remote databases without user intervention. On DOS workstations, SQL*NET runs as a *TSR* (terminate-and-stay-resident) program that works with the networking software to provide access to the ORACLE database. It runs as a *DLL* (dynamic link library) under Windows and OS/2.

ORACLE is the only C/S database besides NetWare SQL to support access from Apple Macintosh clients. When used with TCP/IP, even Unix-based clients can access PC-based ORACLE servers. The SQL*NET drivers take up a moderate amount of RAM, and it's possible to run at least two different versions on the same DOS client (and more on OS/2 or Unix clients). For example, a user can access a NLM database by using NetWare's SPX protocol while simultaneously accessing an OS/2 version by using Microsoft LAN Manager's Named Pipes protocol, provided the workstation has enough available RAM to load both protocols.

SQL*NET 2.0 enhances Oracle's distributed processing capabilities by implementing Oracle's *transparent network substrate* (TNS), a common communications *API* (application program interface) that's protocol-independent. By using TNS-based versions of SQL*NET with Oracle's MultiProtocol Interchange, clients can access different ORACLE databases without regard to the underlying network protocol, and without having to load multiple copies of SQL*NET. SQL*NET 1.0 is included in the ORACLE Server package; version 2.0 is available from Oracle for an additional amount.

Supported Protocols

Versions of SQL*NET 1.0 and 2.0 are available for a number of networking protocols, including:

- *NetBIOS* A standard peer-to-peer protocol developed by IBM and Microsoft.

- *IPX/SPX* Novell's standard networking protocol.

- *Named Pipes* The peer-to-peer protocol developed by Microsoft for the LAN Manager NOS; also used by IBM in its LAN Server NOS.

- *APPC (LU6.2)* The Advanced Peer-to-Peer Communications protocol developed by IBM for communications between clients and large systems, primarily its mainframes.

- *3270* Another name for IBM's SNA network, primarily used to link terminals to its mainframes.

- *DECNet* Digital's standard VAX/VMS networking protocol.

- *TCP/IP*   The Transmission Control Protocol/Internet Protocol that's the standard networking protocol for Unix systems. TCP/IP drivers are available for every platform and network topology available today.

- *Asynchronous*   Client-to-server connections over a standard modem, using the telephone system as the network.

- *X.25*   A *CCITT* (International Telegraph and Telephone Consultative Committee) standard network protocol used over packet-switched networks. X.25 is usually used on dedicated digital telephone links.

SQL*NET is topology-independent. In other words, it doesn't matter which network topology you run it on as long as you're using the proper version of SQL*NET for your network protocol.

Developing Applications with ORACLE's Native Languages

ORACLE's Native Languages

Using SQL with SQL*DBA

Creating Applications with 3GLs

A DBMS IS PRETTY USELESS IF WE DON'T HAVE A WAY TO CREATE AND maintain a database, and enter or update the data in it. To do these things, we need a standard method for talking to the DBMS; in other words, a *programming language*. The programming language lets us send instructions to the DBMS that detail the structure of the database. We also use it to enter data into and retrieve data from the database.

A number of programming languages have been developed over the years. Most computer users have a least a passing knowledge of the common *3GLs* (third-generation languages) such as BASIC, C, and Pascal, which can be used to create any type of program the particular computer can run. 3GLs are general-purpose languages and are not specific to any one type of application.

There's one problem with using a 3GL to create programs that run under a specific type of application. Because 3GLs are general-purpose, they usually don't have commands that perform a particular function in the particular application. This led to the rise of the *4GLs* (fourth-generation languages), which are programming languages specific to a particular application. The majority of 4GLs in existence today are designed for or are part of a particular DBMS. The DBMS's 4GL has commands and statements designed to perform particular functions in that DBMS, making it easier to create database applications.

There are three general types of DBMS 4GLs:

- The first is the group of *proprietary languages*, which are particular to one DBMS. Two examples of a proprietary language are the Paradox Application Language (PAL) used by Borland's Paradox DBMS, and the R/BASIC used by Revelation Technologies' Advanced Revelation.

- The second type of 4GL is one that started out proprietary, but became generally available as other DBMS vendors started including it in their systems. The most common example of this today is the dBASE language; a number of DBMSs are available, in addition to the original dBASE product put out by Borland, that use dBASE-compatible syntax. The most popular are Microsoft's FoxPro and Computer Associates' Clipper. The dBASE language is so popular that efforts are underway to create a standard form of the language; this form is currently referred to as the XBASE language.

- SQL is the third general type of DBMS 4GL. SQL is not restricted to one product or to a group of products; any DMBS can use it. To date, though, SQL is the only DBMS language that has the force of a standard behind it. SQL's standard describes the basic components of the language, and what those components should do. The first SQL standard passed by ANSI came out in 1986 and is referred to as either ANSI SQL-86 or ANSI SQL Level 1. A revised standard was released in 1989 and is referred to as ANSI SQL-89 or ANSI SQL Level 2. The Level 2 standard also includes an addendum that describes commands that govern *referential integrity* (RI), called the Integrity Enhancement addendum.

The majority of RDBMS vendors use SQL as the standard application programming language for their products. However, the standard language is somewhat limited in what it can do, so the vendors also include their own enhancements to tailor SQL to their DBMSs. These enhancements can make different SQL implementations incompatible with each other, requiring application programmers or front-end developers to create and support multiple versions of their products.

ORACLE's Native Languages

Oracle Corp. had the distinction of being the first RDBMS vendor to release a commercial SQL implementation: the ORACLE RDBMS, first released in 1979. ORACLE continues to use SQL as its built-in, or *native*, language for creating and maintaining databases, and for entering and updating data. ORACLE's native SQL is compatible with the ANSI SQL Level 2 standard, and it includes some additional commands that enhance the language beyond what the standard provides for. These additional commands include a number of built-in mathematical and character-string manipulation functions.

ORACLE also comes with *PL/SQL* (Procedural Language/SQL), a superset of the native SQL that includes procedural programming commands for looping, branching, and other program-logic control. Fortunately for ORACLE application developers, both SQL and PL/SQL are compatible across the entire ORACLE line, from the PC version to the mainframe version. Applications created under one version of ORACLE can easily be moved to another.

Version 6.0 of ORACLE includes some command options that fall into the RI category. However, these options are not active in version 6.0 and are present only to provide compatibility with non-ORACLE SQL implementations. Most of these RI options will be functional in version 7.0.

The information provided in the rest of this section on SQL and PL/SQL is primarily for understanding and reference purposes, for running quick ad-hoc queries, or for those building an application from the ground up. One of the advantages of the C/S model is that the application developer generally doesn't have to work directly with either language; the front-end application handles most (if not all) of the necessary translations between its own built-in functions and the ORACLE commands needed to carry out those functions.

SQL Commands, Operators, and Functions

SQL commands can be broken down into three subsets, each of which manages different database functions:

- Data Definition Language (DDL)

- Data Manipulation Language (DML)

- Data Control Language (DCL)

ORACLE supports a fourth SQL subset, called Embedded SQL (EMB).

There are also a number of command operators and functions that can be included in SQL statements. (A *statement* consists of one or more commands, with all the operators the command is to act on.) The commands and functions are usually also keywords, which means that they can't be used for anything but a programming command or statement. For example, you can't use a keyword as the name of a column in a data table. (For more information, see "Operators" and "Functions," later in this chapter.)

There's one more ORACLE SQL command that doesn't fit into any of these four subsets. EXPLAIN PLAN is a tool used by programmers to ask the DBMS how a particular SQL statement will be executed. Application developers can use EXPLAIN PLAN to hand-optimize SQL commands for the best performance on a given database.

The definitions of the four subsets and the SQL commands in those subsets are covered in the following sections. Complete reference information on the syntax of these commands can be found in the *SQL Language Reference* manual included with the ORACLE Server.

Data Definition Language (DDL)

The elements of the DDL are designed for creating and manipulating the schema or structure of a database. Such statements generally start with the keywords ALTER, CREATE, or DROP. Table 3.1 lists the ORACLE SQL commands that fall under the DDL subset.

Table 3.1   **The ORACLE SQL's DDL Commands**

ALTER CLUSTER

ALTER DATABASE

ALTER SEQUENCE

ALTER TABLE

Table 3.1	The ORACLE SQL's DDL Commands (Continued)
	COMMENT
	CREATE DATABASE
	CREATE DATABASE LINK
	CREATE INDEX
	CREATE SEQUENCE
	CREATE SYNONYM
	CREATE TABLE
	CREATE VIEW
	DROP <object>
	RENAME <object>
	VALIDATE INDEX

Data Manipulation Language (DML)

The DML statements let you add to, retrieve, change, and delete the data in the database. ORACLE's DML keywords are listed in Table 3.2.

Table 3.2	The ORACLE SQL's DML Commands
	DELETE
	INSERT
	LOCK TABLE
	SELECT
	UPDATE

Data Control Language (DCL)

The commands in the DCL are used to govern user access to the database, audit database use, and control transaction processing. The DCL also includes any DBMS-specific commands that control setting up and maintaining hard-disk allocation space for the database. ORACLE's DCL commands are listed in Table 3.3. Note that the ORACLE manuals don't distinguish these DCL commands from the DDL and DML statements, improperly listing the commands in Table 3.3 under the other two types.

Table 3.3　**The ORACLE SQL's DCL Commands**

ALTER INDEX

ALTER ROLLBACK SEGMENT

ALTER SESSION

ALTER TABLESPACE

ALTER USER

AUDIT

COMMIT

CREATE CLUSTER

CREATE ROLLBACK SEGMENT

CREATE TABLESPACE

GRANT

NOAUDIT

REVOKE

ROLLBACK

SAVEPOINT

SET TRANSACTION

Embedded SQL (EMB)

The EMB statements are specific to ORACLE, and they are used to place DCL, DDL, and DML commands inside a program created with a 3GL. Using 3GLs to create ORACLE applications is covered later in this chapter. The EMB keywords are listed in Table 3.4.

Table 3.4   **The ORACLE SQL's EMB Commands**

CLOSE <cursor>

CONNECT

DECLARE CURSOR

DECLARE DATABASE

DECLARE STATEMENT

DESCRIBE

EXECUTE

EXECUTE IMMEDIATE

FETCH

OPEN <cursor>

PREPARE

WHENEVER

Operators

Operators are portions of an SQL statement that modify the conditions under which the SQL statement operates. They're usually used to narrow the set or range of data that a particular SQL command covers. Table 3.5 lists the operators that ORACLE supports; full details can be found in the *SQL Language Reference* manual.

Table 3.5   **The ORACLE SQL Operators**

Type	Operator(s)
Arithmetic	()
	+
	−
	*
	/
Character	‖

Table 3.5   The ORACLE SQL Operators (Continued)

Type	Operator(s)
Comparison	()
	=
	!= or ^= or <> (these are interchangeable)
	>=
	<=
	IN
	NOT IN
	ANY
	ALL
	BETWEEN....AND
	NOT BETWEEN....AND
	EXISTS
	NOT EXISTS
	LIKE
	NOT LIKE
	IS NULL
	IS NOT NULL
Logical	()
	NOT
	AND
	OR
Set	UNION
	INTERSECT
	MINUS
Others	(+)
	<table>.*
	COUNT(expr)
	COUNT(*)
	ALL
	DISTINCT
	PRIOR

Functions

Functions are prewritten programming routines that do specific tasks; they're included in a 3GL or 4GL to make the programmer's job easier. ORACLE includes a number of functions that work on numbers, characters or strings, dates, and groups of data. Other functions convert data from one datatype to another, or provide miscellaneous capabilities that don't fall into one of the other categories. Table 3.6 lists all the functions built into ORACLE's SQL implementation.

Table 3.6 **The ORACLE SQL Functions**

Type	Function
Single-Row Number Functions	ABS
	CEIL
	FLOOR
	MOD
	POWER
	ROUND
	SIGN
	SQRT
	TRUNC
Single-Row Character Functions Returning CHAR Values	CHR
	INITCAP
	LOWER
	LPAD
	LTRIM
	REPLACE
	RPAD
	RTRIM
	SOUNDEX
	SUBSTR
	TRANSLATE
	UPPER
Single-Row Character Functions Returning Numeric Values	ASCII
	INSTR
	LENGTH
	NLSSORT
Group Functions	AVG
	COUNT(expr)
	COUNT(*)
	MAX
	MIN
	STDDEV
	SUM
	VARIANCE

Table 3.6 **The ORACLE SQL Functions (Continued)**

Type	Function
Conversion Functions	CHARTOROWID
	CONVERT
	HEXTORAW
	RAWTOHEX
	ROWIDTOCHAR
	TO_CHAR <date conversion>
	TO_CHAR <number conversion>
	TO_DATE
	TO_NUMBER
Date Functions	ADD_MONTHS
	LAST_DAY
	MONTHS_BETWEEN
	NEW_TIME
	NEXT_DAY
	ROUND
	SYSDATE
	TRUNC
Miscellaneous Functions	DECODE
	DUMP
	GREATEST
	LEAST
	NVL
	UID
	USER
	USERENV
	VSIZE

PL/SQL

PL/SQL is primarily an application development language that adds a number of procedural non-SQL statements to the built-in SQL. It's usually used to add SQL statements to programs written in a 3GL, using one of the ORACLE precompilers (discussed in the last section of this chapter).

The biggest advantage of PL/SQL is that it groups SQL commands, operators, and functions into a block that can be sent to the RDBMS as a single unit. Standard SQL statements are sent to the RDBMS one at a time, which increases both the traffic on the network and the processing overhead at the server. PL/SQL blocks reduce network traffic by sending all the statements at once, and then waiting for the RDBMS's response.

On the other hand, PL/SQL doesn't support any of the DDL statements and also doesn't support the DCL statements CONNECT, GRANT, and RE-VOKE. These statements have to be entered directly through a utility that doesn't process or alter the SQL before sending it to the DBMS. An example of this type of utility is the SQL*DBA program included with the ORACLE Server.

PL/SQL is the basis for the ORACLE Tools, a set of application development tools put out by Oracle Corp. (these are covered in Chapter 4). Most third-party front ends also use PL/SQL as the basis for their ORACLE interfaces. Table 3.7 lists the PL/SQL commands. Full details can be found in the *PL/SQL User's Guide and Reference* manual, included with the ORACLE Server.

Table 3.7	**ORACLE PL/SQL Commands**
	BEGIN
	CLOSE
	COMMIT
	DECLARE <object>
	DELETE
	END
	EXCEPTION
	EXCEPTION_INIT
	EXIT
	FETCH
	GOTO
	IF...THEN...ELSEIF..ELSE
	INSERT
	LOCK TABLE
	LOOP
	NULL
	OPEN
	RAISE

Table 3.7	**ORACLE PL/SQL Commands (Continued)**
	ROLLBACK
	SAVEPOINT
	SELECT....INTO
	SET TRANSACTION
	UPDATE

Using SQL with SQL*DBA

In addition to its database administration and monitoring capabilities, the character-mode SQL*DBA utility included with the ORACLE Server lets the DBA and users directly enter and execute SQL statements and its own internal commands. PL/SQL commands can also be executed by the SQL*DBA; however, because of their procedural nature, they can be executed only as part of a text file, and not directly entered. Table 3.8 lists the additional commands supported by the SQL*DBA. Note that the commands that are followed by a double asterisk (**) are restricted to the DBA; all others can be utilized by any user. Full syntax for the SQL*DBA commands can be found in Appendix A of the *Database Administrator's Guide* that comes with the ORACLE Server.

Table 3.8	**SQL*DBA Additional Commands**
	ARCHIVE LOG
	CONNECT <database>
	CONNECT INTERNAL **
	DISCONNECT
	EXIT
	MONITOR
	RECOVER
	REMARK
	SET <ORACLE Environment variable>
	SHOW

Table 3.8	**SQL*DBA Additional Commands (Continued)**
	SHUTDOWN**
	SPOOL
	STARTUP **

** indicates commands restricted to those with DBA authorization

Interactive Commands

Figure 3.1 shows the start of an SQL*DBA session under OS/2. After the program is executed, the current-version information is displayed, and the prompt changes to

```
SQLDBA>
```

(SQLDBA is the actual name of the program in this case, as well as under DOS). Commands are entered directly at the prompt. Shown here are the commands that enter the DBA's password, and the command to start the ORACLE Server.

Figure 3.1
The initial SQL*DBA screen. The commands shown enter the DBA's password and start the ORACLE Server.

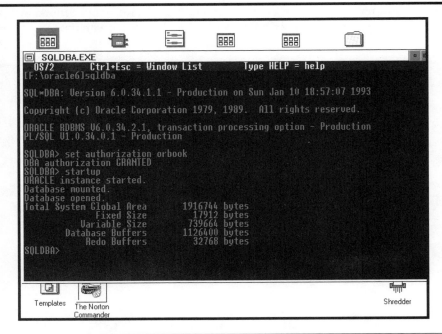

There are several ways to execute directly entered statements in SQL*DBA:

- If the statement is a SQL*DBA command, simply type the command and press Enter. The command will be executed immediately. For example, the command to connect to a database called BOOKTEST would look like this:

```
SQLDBA> connect booktest <ENTER>
```

Note that SQL*DBA statements are case-insensitive.

- Direct SQL commands must be entered a bit differently. SQL*DBA needs to know that you've finished entering the SQL statement, so it can process and execute it. There are two ways of doing so.

- The first, used for SQL statements that fit on a single line, is to end the statement with a semicolon and hit Enter, like this:

```
SQLDBA> SELECT Name, Address, SSN FROM EMPLOYEES; <ENTER>
```

- The second method, which can be used for single lines or for SQL statements that extend over multiple lines, is to put a forward slash (/) on a line all by itself. The command would then look like this:

```
SQLDBA> SELECT Name, Address, City, State, Zip
     2> FROM EMPLOYEES
     3> / <ENTER>
```

- The final way to execute a single SQL*DBA command is by entering the command on the SQL*DBA command line when starting the program. This is done by adding COMMAND="command string" (with the quotation marks) after SQLDBA at the prompt. For example, you could automatically enter your password every time you start SQL*DBA by putting the following on the command line:

```
C:> SQLDBA COMMAND="SET AUTHORIZATION ORBOOK"
```

Commands Stored in Text Files

Entering commands interactively is fine if you're running them only once. However, it can get pretty tedious to enter the same commands over and over again every time you need to run them. There's a simple solution to this: Put the commands in an ASCII text file, and then run the file from SQL*DBA. The syntax is simple:

```
SQLDBA> @filename
```

SQL*DBA assumes that the file extension is .SQL unless you tell it otherwise. The same rules for entering SQL statements apply in a text file as they do interactively. End the statement in a semicolon, or with a forward slash on the same line or alone on the next line.

This capability is very handy, as it also lets ORACLE users easily share SQL programs that are compatible across the entire ORACLE line. There are a number of handy SQL programs and utilities written by other ORACLE users, available for downloading from the file libraries of CompuServe's ORACLE Forum.

Creating Applications with 3GLs

Writing a long and complex database application as a text file can be a daunting undertaking. Plus, SQL and PL/SQL can't control the screen or ask the user for input. To take advantage of these advanced and usually machine-specific functions requires the application developer to create a full-fledged program. Such programs can be written directly with a 3GL, or by using an application development toolkit or front-end package. The trend today is decidedly toward using toolkits and front ends, but there are occasions when a developer needs a program that's too complex to write under the SQL*DBA, but too simple for the overhead the toolkits or front ends entail.

And, of course, anyone writing a new ORACLE front end needs to use a 3GL to create it, and also to translate the user's requests to the SQL and PL/SQL commands and statements that are sent to the RDBMS.

Oracle provides two different methods of including ORACLE SQL and PL/SQL commands in a 3GL application: the *ORACLE Call Interface* (OCI) and the *ORACLE Precompiler*. The OCI is the more machine-specific of the two, and is shipped as a set of runtime libraries for the particular 3GL compiler you're using. The OCI includes specialized versions of the SQL and PL/SQL commands, as well as other commands for the particular 3GL, which makes it easy to integrate custom applications with an ORACLE Server. The OCI is primarily aimed at developers writing sophisticated applications from the ground up. The *Programmer's Guide to the ORACLE Call Interfaces* contains details on all the OCI functions and routines.

Supported Languages

OCI libraries are available for Ada, C, COBOL, FORTRAN, and PL/I. At least one OCI library comes with the ORACLE Server, depending on the target operating system. For example, the NetWare and OS/2 ORACLE Servers come with the C OCI libraries for the Microsoft C compiler.

Precompilers are available for Ada, C, COBOL, FORTRAN, Pascal, and PL/I. However, they're not all available for all the operating systems ORA-CLE supports. Again, the NetWare and OS/2 versions of ORACLE come with the C precompiler. (For more information, see the next section, which covers the ORACLE precompiler.)

Oracle calls its 3GL interfaces Pro*<language>, such as Pro*C, or Pro*-COBOL. Libraries for languages other than the one included in the package are available from Oracle for an additional charge. Supplemental manuals explain the various Pro* interfaces and libraries, and how to use them.

The ORACLE Precompiler

The ORACLE precompiler is a powerful programming tool that lets application developers add embedded SQL and PL/SQL statements directly to a program written with a 3GL. The precompiler examines the SQL statements in the source code, and then translates them into native-language ORACLE calls that use the ORACLE runtime library. The precompiler then creates a separate library that's combined with the rest of the program. This saves the application programmer from the tedious task of manually formatting the SQL statements into a form the compiler can use.

Also important is the precompiler's support for dynamic SQL. Standard embedded SQL statements contain all the information the program needs to execute them, and they don't need different values or parameters every time the program containing them is run. Dynamic SQL statements are built at runtime and can be different for each execution. Dynamic SQL lets the program take input from the user and use that input as the parameters for the SQL command. It even lets the user enter complete SQL statements. The precompiler lets the developer include dynamic SQL support in the application without causing errors when the program is compiled. Creating a program that uses dynamic SQL is a complex process, but doing so gives the application developer complete flexibility when designing the user interface. Just about all of the third-party front ends rely on dynamic SQL to create complex applications.

Finally, the precompiler makes it easier to port programs from one environment to another. The programmer has only to modify the portions of the 3GL that are different for the new environment, and run the precompiler for that environment against the source code. The precompiler takes care of resolving SQL and PL/SQL statements and calls to the new runtime library. The *Programmer's Guide to the ORACLE Precompilers*, included with every ORACLE Server, explains how to use the different precompilers and how to add dynamic SQL statements to an application. Supplemental manuals are also available for using the various Pro* 3GL interfaces with the precompiler.

4

Application
Development Tools

THERE'S A BETTER WAY TO DEVELOP AND PROGRAM THE VAST MAJORITY of front-end applications than to write code in a 3GL. By using an application development tool, the process of creating a C/S application can be greatly simplified. *Application development tools,* or *toolkits,* are software packages specifically designed to create front-end applications that can be run as they are, or further customized by the programmer before being distributed to the end users.

Application development tools take much of the drudgery out of creating applications, by taking care of some or all of the lower-level program code that interfaces the application to the hardware or database server. By doing this, the tools give the application developer more time to concentrate on the design of the application itself, and on its user interface.

Using a toolkit can also significantly reduce the amount of time needed to design and develop the final application. A major part of the costs associated with any computerized system is the personnel costs in time and benefits. Using application development tools to reduce these costs helps make the whole system (hardware and software) more cost-effective.

Evaluating Application Development Tools

Deciding which C/S application development tool is right for your needs is a pretty straightforward process. There are a number already on the market, and new ones are constantly being released. The balance of this chapter will cover the more common ones; if a product you're interested in is not here, you can use the information in this section as a starting point to evaluate if the product fits your needs.

Hardware and Operating System Support

The main thing you need to know before purchasing a toolkit is whether it supports your hardware and operating system. This is particularly critical if you have a mixed environment, with Intel-based PCs, Macintoshes, and Unix workstations that need to access the database. The odds are that most application development tools only support one environment each, so you'll have to use more than one to develop applications for the different platforms. Fortunately, the vast majority of user systems in businesses today are based on the Intel CPUs, so you shouldn't have too many problems finding a variety of toolkits to choose from. You should also be aware of what basic hardware system you require; as application programs become more complex, it's not unusual for a toolkit to require a minimum-level processor, such as an 80286 or even an 80386, and a minimum amount of RAM in which to run. Make sure your development systems have the resources needed by the application development tool you're evaluating.

Considering the User Interface

After determining whether the toolkit will support your hardware and operating system, the next step is to decide which of the many user interfaces you want to create applications for. Macintosh users don't have a choice, as the *GUI* (graphical user interface) is the only one available. Users of Intel-based PCs and Unix systems have more options. The most common interface today is still the character-mode (text) interface, represented by MS-DOS and PC-DOS in the Intel world, and straight Unix. GUIs are rapidly becoming more popular, and you may have decided to move your users to one. In this case, you have the choice between Microsoft Windows 3.1 and IBM OS/2 2.0 Presentation Manager for Intel systems, and Unix-based GUIs such as Motif and Open Look for workstations. By the end of 1993, Microsoft Windows NT should also be available. Windows NT is slated to run on a number of platforms, including Intel-based systems and various RISC workstations.

Application development tools are particularly important for a GUI-based system, as the toolkit usually handles the details of creating applications that run under the particular GUI; this relieves the programmer from possibly having to learn a whole new way of creating user interface screens.

Five Important Questions to Ask

Here are some questions you should ask about the products you're considering:

- **What 3GL does the toolkit use?** It's important to chose a toolkit that uses a language your programmers are familiar with. This is especially true if you expect to create or use customized routines as part of your applications. Having to learn a new language increases the amount of time a programmer needs to design and develop an application.

  However, many application development tools use their own built-in language and don't interface with any external 3GLs. While these languages are usually very powerful and quite capable of creating complex applications, you should be aware that additional time will be needed to learn the new language.

- **Does the toolkit create standalone applications?** It's important to know if the final application can be compiled and run on its own, or if you have to buy a copy of the development environment for every user. This can greatly affect the final cost of the application. On the plus side, standalone executables prevent the end users from inadvertently changing the source code. Also, they usually execute faster, because the optimization is done by the compiler.

Some toolkits provide a half-way solution, called a runtime module or runtime program. A *runtime module* is a limited version of the full development environment that's designed only to run applications from their source code, or from a binary compiled format. While not as convenient as standalone executables, runtime modules make it easier to distribute applications than to run them under the full environment.

- **Are there any additional licensing costs?** Some vendors provide the developer with an unlimited license to distribute applications created with that company's toolkit. Others require a license fee for each copy of the final application distributed; this is more common with vendors that provide runtime modules instead of compiling the application into a standalone executable. (Some vendors license the application executables on a per-server basis.) The basic-configuration cost of the application development toolkit may only include a license for a single user or a limited number of users of the runtime module. If this is the case, you may suddenly find yourself laying out much more money than you anticipated for legally distributing the application among your users.

- **Does the toolkit work with other database servers besides ORACLE?** It's not uncommon for a company to use more than one vendor's database server, especially if the computing environment consists of a mixture of microcomputers, minicomputers, and mainframes. If you need to access more than one database server with the same or similar applications, make sure the application development tool you choose supports the others.

- **What are the toolkit vendor's support policies?** The best application development tools in the world are no good to you if you can't get support when you need it. Unfortunately, many vendors' support policies still consist of providing only a limited period of free support during normal business hours—*its* normal hours, not yours. If you anticipate needing support during any hour of the day or night, make sure the vendor provides support 24 hours a day, 7 days a week. Also find out the vendor's options for extended support beyond the usual free period. Such support usually costs more, but in the long run it can be cheaper than the internal costs you face when a critical computer system goes down for extended periods.

ORACLE Tools and Other Oracle Design Aids

As can be expected, Oracle Corp. has a wide variety of application development tools available for creating applications for its RDBMS. Some of these toolkits are still designed primarily for creating central host applications that are accessed through terminals, so we won't be concerning ourselves with them here.

However, Oracle does have a couple of toolkits available that will create either central host or C/S applications. Chief among these are SQL*Forms, SQL*Menu, SQL*ReportWriter, and SQL*TextRetrieval. Oracle bundles the first three into a single package called ORACLE Tools.

SQL*Forms

SQL*Forms is probably the most useful and popular tool available from Oracle. With SQL*Forms, the developer can create a complete form-based user interface to the database, making it easy for the user to enter, search for, or update data. Forms can be used as part of an application running on a central host, or as part of a front-end application in a C/S system.

Each form is composed of a number of objects:

- Blocks: Sections or subsections of the form. A form can contain one or more blocks, with each block associated with a particular database or view.

- Fields: Columns for display, or data entry areas. Each form field can describe the format of how the data should be displayed to the user. Form fields can also have data validation rules associated with them, which ensure that the data entered into the field fits within a predetermined set or range of values.

- Pages: Non-modifiable display areas on a form. Pages can be used to display constant text, such as help text for the user, or to display a range of valid data values for a particular field. Multiple pages can be simultaneously visible on the user's screen. The developer has complete control over the size of the page, and whether it should automatically pop up for the user.

- Triggers: Processing routines associated with a particular event in a form. Triggers are PL/SQL routines that the developer can use to automate certain functions; for example, a trigger can automatically close and disconnect any open databases when the user exits from the form. Triggers can also be associated with certain keystrokes, depending on the platform on which the form is running. For example, different triggers can be associated with the function keys on an IBM PC so the routines are executed when the user presses a specific key.

- Form-level procedures: Processing commands that are global to a single form. Form-level procedures are similar to triggers, in that they're usually written in PL/SQL. However, form-level procedures are global in scope and are not associated with a particular event or keystroke. These procedures are commonly used as a type of program library for a particular form, as they represent standard routines that can be called from other form-level procedures or triggers. Form-level procedures can save programmers a lot of time and effort, as they reduce the need for constantly rewriting the same programming code in every separate trigger.

SQL*Forms and SQL*Menu are designed to work closely together.

SQL*Menu

SQL*Menu is a system of components that are used to design, create, and run various types of user application menus. The menu items themselves can call PL/SQL procedures, bring up forms created with SQL*Forms or reports created with SQL*ReportWriter, or call various submenus for further user action. Menu items can even be used to start external programs. User access to different portions of the menu application can be controlled by the DBA, which lets the developer design a single menu application for all users, and present only the relevant parts of the menu to the user, based on the user's security privileges.

The main SQL*Menu interface consists of four components:

- Design: Used to define and modify menu applications. It can also be used by DBAs to control user security and access to applications through SQL*Menu.

- Generate: Creates the actual program-code library from the menu design created with the design component.

- Document: Creates a text file that stores information about the menu design.

- Run: Used by users to run the menu application.

Menus can have one of several appearance styles. The standard style is a *pull-down menu*, where user choices drop down from a main menu bar that runs across the top of the screen. A similar menu style is the *bar menu*, where all menu items (including submenu choices) appear as a single bar across the top of the screen. Users make their selections by moving the highlight bar and pressing Enter.

The third type is the *full-screen menu,* where each menu item appears on a single line centered in the middle of the screen. Users can use the highlight bar to make their choices, or enter the menu item in a dialog box.

SQL*ReportWriter

SQL*ReportWriter is a full-screen interactive report-design tool. It lets the developer create free-form reports that can include one or more fields from the database. Items in the report can be grouped together based on a common value, and breakpoints can be established to create subtotals based on a group.

SQL*ReportWriter includes a number of built-in summary functions, which are listed in Table 4.1. The report writer automatically provides forward referencing, which lets the designer print the summary of a group of items before the items themselves are displayed. The report designer can also create other functions for particular circumstances by creating a PL/SQL routine and assigning it to a particular summary field.

Table 4.1   SQL*ReportWriter Standard Summary Functions

Avg (average)

Count

First

Last

Max (maximum)

Min (minimum)

%Total

Sum

Reports can be run from within forms created by SQL*Forms, or directly from the command line by using the RUNREP runtime utility included in the package. Menus created with SQL*Menu can run reports by calling the runtime module.

Reports, forms, and menus created with these three design tools can also be accessed and run from programs created in a 3GL. Supported 3GLs include Ada, C, COBOL, FORTRAN, Pascal, and PL/I.

SQL*Plus

ORACLE Tools also includes a program called SQL*Plus, which is an enhanced version of the SQL*DBA included in the ORACLE Server package. Like SQL*DBA, SQL*Plus is an interactive character-mode utility that lets the user directly enter SQL and PL/SQL commands at the SQL> prompt, or run a text file that contains SQL or PL/SQL commands. The main enhancement SQL*PLUS brings to the character-mode interface is the ability to format the output from SELECT commands, making the output easier to read.

SQL*TextRetrieval

SQL*TextRetrieval is a separate toolkit that extends ORACLE's built-in SQL and better manages data stored as text. SQL*TextRetrieval primarily works with the CHAR and LONG datatypes. It also adds a CONTAINS keyword parameter to the built-in SQL that lets the user search a text field based on a portion of the text stored in the field.

SQL*TextRetrieval creates a separate text index to speed searches through large databases. It works from within SQL*Forms, and it can also be interfaced to the same 3GLs as the application development tools included in ORACLE Tools.

Supported Platforms

SQL*Forms, SQL*Menu, SQL*ReportWriter, and SQL*TextRetrieval have one big advantage over the other application development tools discussed in this chapter: They're available for every platform the ORACLE RDBMS runs on. The forms, reports, and menus created with these tools are completely portable between the different platforms, making ORACLE Tools the best choice for mixed computing environments.

SQL*Forms and SQL*Menu also come in versions that support some of the GUIs available, including the OS/2 Presentation Manager, Macintosh, and Unix Motif environments. SQL*ReportWriter can be used in conjunction with the SQL*Connect packages to create reports from databases in IBM's DB2 and SQL/DS, as well as other DBMSs supported by SQL*Connect versions.

SQLWindows

Gupta Technologies is best know for its SQLBase database server. However, it also sells two popular front-end products that support its own RDBMS and others, including ORACLE. The first is SQLWindows, an application development tool that assists programmers in creating Windows 3.x–based client applications. The second is a query and reporting tool called Quest, which I'll be covering further in Chapter 6.

SQLWindows, version 3.0, can be used either as a user query tool or an application development platform. Gupta includes a single-user version of its

SQLBase DBMS in the package, allowing developers to create front-end applications for their own RDBMSs without needing a full C/S system. SQLWindows isn't limited to supporting only SQLBase, though; developers can use it to create front ends for ORACLE, Microsoft SQL Server, Sybase SQL Server, INGRES, IBM's OS/2 Database Manager and SQL/400, NetWare SQL, and Hewlett-Packard's AllBase. Different database servers can be accessed from the same application, which makes SQLWindows useful in a mixed environment.

The Programming Environment

SQLWindows' programming environment is object-oriented, but it isn't as tightly integrated as others, such as Powersoft Corp.'s PowerBuilder (discussed in the next section). In addition to supporting direct SQL statements, SQLWindows includes its own SQL Windows Application Language (SAL). There's no support for integrating SQLWindows applications with those created in a 3GL.

As Figure 4.1 shows, SQLWindows uses a series of separate windows on the Windows 3.*x* desktop for designing and creating the application. SQLWindows lets you use a separate window to monitor the programming code that it's creating. It adds the appropriate SAL statements to the program each time the developer adds or modifies an object on the design screen.

SQL*Windows also has debugging capabilities built-in, and the developer can create a runtime application file that's used with the runtime module to execute the application outside of SQLWindows.

SQLWindows includes a couple of modules that let developers and users create front-end applications without having to write program code. Express Windows is used to create an on-screen form or table view of the database, and ReportWindows lets the developer create custom reports by painting the design on the screen. SQLWindows also provides Windows Dynamic Data Exchange (DDE) support so that data can be shared automatically with other Windows applications, such as a spreadsheet or charting program.

Release of Version 4.0

In the second quarter of 1993, Gupta will be releasing version 4.0 of SQLWindows, which has many significant enhancements over the current version. Chief among them is a collaborative programming environment Gupta calls TeamWindows, available in the Corporate Edition. TeamWindows makes it easier for a team of application developers to work on the same application, by providing the following:

- An application generator.

Figure 4.1

Gupta's SQLWindows isn't a tightly integrated development environment. The main window (titled SQLWindows here) shows you the SAL code being written as you add various objects to the design screen (bottom window).

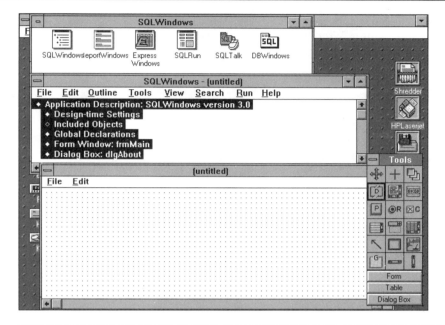

■ Security features that keep track of which programmer accesses which code module.

■ Source-code–version management and control.

Another new feature is the inclusion of QuestWindow, which adds the quick query functions of Gupta's Quest to SQLWindows. These query functions can be used as a quick prototyping tool by the programmer, to ensure that the SQL statements included in the application are correct and returning the proper results. A QuestWindow browse or edit window can also be included as part of an application, to provide the end-user with ad hoc query capabilities.

Finally, version 4.0 adds complete support for the new features introduced in Windows 3.1, including the Multiple Document Interface (MDI), which makes it easier to have multiple windows open from within the same application; and Object Linking and Embedding (OLE), which provides the ability to include other applications (such as a charting program) or objects directly in a SQLWindows application. An application included through OLE is automatically executed when the user accesses the SQLWindows form or screen that the external application is linked to.

Supported Platforms

As I mentioned previously, SQLWindows is only available for systems running Windows 3.*x*. No other versions are available at this time, and Gupta has not publicly stated any plans for supporting other GUIs.

PowerBuilder

SQLWindows' closest competitor is Powersoft's Windows-based Power-Builder. Both are very popular among C/S application developers, and additional support is available from various user groups.

PowerBuilder is a powerful object-oriented front-end developer toolkit that's aimed primarily at the corporate and MIS applications programmer. In addition to ORACLE, it supports the Microsoft SQL Server and Sybase SQL Server, Gupta's SQLBase, XDB System's xdb-DBMS, INGRES, HP's All-Base, and IBM's DB2. The developer's package comes with support for one of these servers; additional server interfaces are available at extra cost.

PowerBuilder has no native database manager, and it requires a connection to a database server to build and test applications. As with SQLWindows, an application can connect to more than one database server at the same time. It takes full advantage of the Windows 3.*x* environment; all development is done through *painters*, which is the PowerBuilder name for the various modules that are used to create the database; define the menus and screen appearance; manipulate the data; and develop, debug, and maintain applications (see Figure 4.2). While the module's icons are displayed separately on the main menu, they're also tightly linked and can be executed from within each other as the need arises.

PowerBuilder includes two additional tools to make application development easier. The Library module is used to maintain application libraries, which can be browsed, separated, merged, or regenerated, and it can also create a full report on a library's contents. The Debug module is a full debugger that supports single-step processing and breakpoints. It can be run on its own or from the various painters during the development process. The only elements PowerBuilder lacks are a robust report writer and a tool that creates graphs based on the data.

Powersoft has announced that it will support version 7.0 of ORACLE as soon as it's released for the common C/S platforms. The SQL connection modules for version 7.0 are currently in late beta testing, which means that Powersoft may well be the first third-party vendor to provide support for the new version.

Figure 4.2

PowerBuilder includes application development tools that Powersoft calls painters. Developers will find it a tightly integrated object-oriented development environment.

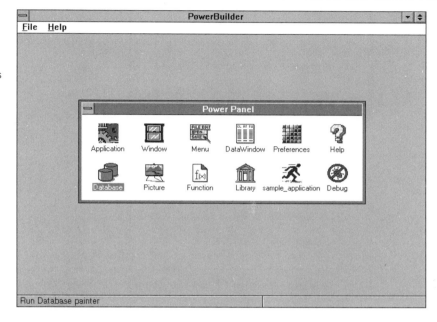

The Programming Environment

Underlying all the modules and tying the development environment together is PowerScript, PowerBuilder's C-like script language. While prior knowledge of C or SQL isn't necessary to create applications in PowerBuilder, an understanding of the event and message-passing nature of Windows applications, as well as a knowledge of object-oriented programming techniques, helps smooth the development process. PowerScript's similarity to C also makes it easier for a 3GL programmer to adapt quickly to its development environment. The included manuals do discuss the event, message-passing, and object-oriented concepts briefly, and they include many examples of the proper use of PowerScript statements and functions.

The DataWindow Painter

The DataWindow Painter, the heart of PowerBuilder, is its most powerful feature. It's used in combination with SQL statements or PowerScript scripts to retrieve and manipulate one or more rows of data from the database server. Data can be displayed in tabular rows, or in a free-form window created by the Window Painter. SQL statements can be custom-written or built through the SQL Painter, and the PowerScript Painter is used to create script files, drawing from over 70 built-in functions. User-defined functions are also supported and can be created through the Function Painter. Full DDE support is included, and external Windows or database-server library functions can be called from within a script.

Incorporating Windows Graphics

When the development is completed, the developer uses the built-in compiler to compile the application into a runtime application file composed of Windows dynamic link libraries (DLLs). When combined with the PowerBuilder runtime module, the application can be used independent of the developer environment.

PowerBuilder makes excellent use of Windows graphics throughout the entire development process; for example, a key icon is attached to the appropriate columns to indicate on which column the table is indexed, and a view icon is connected to the tables that are part of a view. Bitmapped graphics files (created externally or through the Picture Painter) can also be associated with a column in a database, regardless of the database server; the bitmap's filename is stored as the data in the column, and the bitmap is displayed by PowerBuilder when the row is retrieved.

The database server can also be administered through PowerBuilder; the developer can enter SQL statements that are sent directly to the server to maintain users, groups, and security, and execute stored procedures (if supported by the particular database server). PowerBuilder makes it easy to create common SQL statements through the SQL Painter, which builds the statements through point-and-shoot pick lists.

Supported Platforms

Currently the only supported platform is Windows 3.x. Powersoft is investigating creating a version of PowerBuilder for OS/2 2.0, but it has not announced firm plans or a release date at this time.

ObjectVision

Borland started out as a 3GL compiler vendor, and it has grown to be one of the major vendors of software for Intel-based microcomputers. ObjectVision is the latest in its long line of application development and programming environments.

ObjectVision is a GUI-based application development environment, with versions available for Windows 3.x and OS/2 2.0. Its primary developer and user interface is based on on-screen forms, using object-oriented techniques to create the application. The Design mode is used by the developer to create the overall forms and any objects on the forms, such as text, dialog boxes, and data fields.

The Design mode uses a visual editor that creates an on-screen flowchart to describe the steps taken by the application. The various steps are linked to forms that are also created on-screen through a form editor. No traditional programming is required, and in fact ObjectVision doesn't even include a scripting or programming language. No support is provided for accessing ObjectVision forms from within 3GL programs. Forms can be linked to other forms, and data can also be passed from a form to another Windows application through DDE and OLE. Because of its screen-oriented approach to development, ObjectVision can even be used by non-programmers to create sophisticated C/S front-end applications.

The Form Completion mode, which executes the completed application, is the interface the end user of the application actually sees. Borland includes a runtime module that carries no additional licensing fees, and lets developers freely distribute completed applications.

The base-priced ObjectVision package provides direct support for accessing data from Borland's Paradox DBMS, any dBASE-compatible data files, and data files that use the NetWare BTrieve data engine. Links to database servers are provided by ObjectVision SQL Connection, a version of the SQL Link package used by Borland's Paradox to connect to external RDBMSs. In addition to ORACLE, SQL Connection provides access to IBM's OS/2 Database Manager and DB2, Microsoft SQL Server and Sybase SQL Server, and Digital's VAX Rdb/VMS 4.1. Each SQL Connection package supports only one database server, but multiple connections can be made by using multiple packages.

Supported Platforms

Versions of ObjectVision are available for both Windows 3.*x* and OS/2 2.0. Also available is a bundled package called ObjectVision Pro, a complete C/S application development system that includes ObjectVision, a SQL Connection module, and a copy of Turbo C++ for Windows. At this time, the Pro version is only available for Windows 3.*x*.

Object/1

Micro Data Base Systems is best known as the vendor of two microcomputer and minicomputer DBMSs—MDBS IV and KnowledgeMan—as well as the expert system-development package, GURU. MDBS also sells Object/1, an object-oriented, graphical database-application builder.

Object/1 was originally released as a database development toolkit for the OS/2 Presentation Manager. A version for Windows 3.x has since been released. The base-priced package supports creating GUI applications for MDBS's two database products; access to ORACLE is provided through the Object/1 Professional Pack. Microsoft SQL Server, Sybase SQL Server, and IBM's Database Manager are also supported through other Professional Packs.

Object/1 is primarily aimed at non-programmers, even though it contains a full object-oriented programming language that resembles C++. Its components are all screen-oriented, so the developer has only to create the elements on the screen, and Object/1 will create the appropriate source code. A database engine based on MDBS IV is included in the package, so standalone applications can be created in addition to those that access a database server.

The Forms Painter is the primary interface and is used to create all the objects the user will see on the screen. A floating pallet lists all the available objects, and makes it easy to place them on the form.

Other modules include the System Browser, which lets the programmer search for particular code modules in the source code and edit them. The Project Browser is related to the System Browser; it decomposes a complete application into smaller pieces for testing and editing. A full debugging tool is also included.

Unfortunately, Object/1 doesn't include any type of runtime module, so the whole package is needed to run applications developed under it. The final cost of the application can rise quickly if you have a significant number of users to support, especially when you add in the extra cost for the Professional Packs needed.

Supported Platforms

Versions of the Object/1 and Object/1 Professional packs are available for OS/2 and Windows 3.x. The OS/2 version is still based on OS/2 1.3, so it's limited to creating 16-bit applications. However, the OS/2 applications will run under OS/2 2.0, so this limitation isn't very serious.

A Word about Database-Independent APIs

The proliferation of different RDBMSs from the various vendors has resulted in a number of efforts to create a common, database-independent application programming interface (API). A common API would make it easier for developers and vendors of front-end applications to support any number of database servers, without having to write specific drivers for each RDBMS. Ironically, at this time there are four competing versions of a common API, each with its own backers and capabilities.

While the idea of a database-independent API is noble, the reality we have today is no different than the situation that exists between the competing database servers. With the exception of EDA/SQL, every vendor has its own agenda in pushing its own API as the standard, and the marketplace and intercompany politics are the driving forces behind which standard other vendors end up supporting. I very much doubt that we'll see a single standard develop within the next several years, or even before the end of the decade. In the meantime, the front-end application developers continue to be caught in the middle, hoping that they chose the right API to support.

Open Database Connectivity (ODBC)

The first common API was the Microsoft Open Database Connectivity (ODBC) API. ODBC allows developers to talk to the ODBC driver, and the driver handles the translations needed to access the back-end database in its own language. While support is gaining for ODBC, there is one problem keeping it from becoming the overwhelming standard. Microsoft provides ODBC drivers for its own database products; other RDBMS vendors have to write their own ODBC interface for their own products. Many are reluctant to do so until a clear standard develops, or until support for ODBC reaches a critical mass. This problem isn't limited to ODBC, though, as other DBMS vendors have also released their own common APIs, and they are reluctant to support a competitor's. At this time, there is no ODBC driver for ORACLE.

EDA/SQL

Information Builders has taken a slightly different approach from Microsoft with its Enterprise Data Access/SQL (EDA/SQL) common API. EDA/SQL uses a gateway system to access over 50 different DBMSs, including ORACLE. A *gateway system* is a type of database server that doesn't actually store any data; instead, it processes incoming EDA/SQL statements, determines the destination database server, and translates the statements into the appropriate SQL dialect. It also handles any data translations needed between the front-end application and the database server. The gateway is completely independent of whatever platform the database server is running on, provided both can use a common network protocol to communicate.

Information Builders doesn't sell a database server, so its product is independent of any one back end. The company has also taken it on itself to write the interfaces for the different DBMSs, instead of leaving the job to the vendors. Because of this, EDA/SQL currently has the best potential to become the standard cross-platform database API.

Integrated Database API (IDAPI)

At the 1992 Fall Comdex show in Las Vegas, Borland, IBM, Novell, and WordPerfect announced the Integrated Database API (IDAPI), a competitor to ODBC. The full IDAPI specifications will be released sometime in mid-1993. Initially, IDAPI will support databases created by Borland's dBASE, Paradox, and Interbase database server, as well as IBM's Database Manager, NetWare BTrieve, NetWare SQL, and WordPerfect's DataPerfect database. Other companies that announced support for IDAPI include Gupta (SQL-Base Server), XDB Systems (xdb-DBMS), and Microrim (R:BASE). As with ODBC, it remains to be seen how many DBMS and front-end vendors will provide support for IDAPI.

Oracle Glue

Not to be outdone, Oracle Corp. announced its own common API for accessing various DBMSs, calling it Oracle Glue. Oracle Glue is designed to provide developers of Windows-based front ends with a common API for accessing data residing on an ORACLE Server, as well as in dBASE and Paradox files. Oracle has also announced that the initial version of Glue, which is in beta testing at the time of this writing, will support IBM's DB2 and SQL/DS. A later release will add support for the Sybase SQL Server and ODBC. The initial version is due to be released sometime in the second quarter of 1993.

I find it interesting that Oracle decided to add ODBC support to Glue, instead of supporting ODBC directly. While this may be an attempt to cover all the bases, the additional overhead involved in going through two separate translation processes may well be enough to make the Glue-to-ODBC link virtually unusable.

CHAPTER

5

Front-End Add-ons to Existing Products

A MAJOR ADVANTAGE OF THE CLIENT/SERVER ARCHITECTURE IS FRONT-end independence; you're not limited to using only the database manager's built-in application design language and user interface, as you are with a DBMS like dBASE. This is particularly true when it comes to connecting the applications you already use to a database server. As C/S databases increase in popularity, more and more software vendors are providing built-in or optional drivers that link their applications to the server for queries, updates, and data imports.

There are many good reasons for using an existing application to access a database server. The most important involves training; since your users and programmers are already familiar with the application, only a modest amount of training (if any) is needed to get them up to speed on the additional capabilities provided by the database link. Another important reason is the ability to combine existing data stored in local databases or spreadsheets with the data stored on the server. You may also have a significant amount of data in an existing database; an add-on lets you gradually move from a traditional multiuser DBMS to a C/S system.

On the other hand, there's usually additional overhead involved in using an application not explicitly designed to act as a client. The overhead of translating the application's native-language statements into the SQL the server understands can have a significant impact on performance, as can translating the data received in response to the query into a format the application can use.

If you keep the limitations in mind, though, using a familiar application to access a C/S database is a reasonable compromise between utility and performance. This type of setup may be the best available for casual or light database server access needs.

Evaluating Add-ons

It's only natural that the majority of add-ons exist for PC-based databases; after all, the majority of client systems are PCs based on Intel chips, and just about every organization that has PCs also has PC databases. PC database vendors are very eager to make sure their products continue to be useful (and purchased) as more and more businesses move to the C/S architecture.

Deciding whether or not to use an existing application as a front end to a C/S database is a pretty simple process. Many spreadsheet and PC-based database products have drivers for one or more database servers, including ORACLE. The first and most important question is, are the necessary drivers for the link to an ORACLE database available? If the answer to this question is yes, you can then evaluate whether using an existing application fits your needs.

The simplest way to do this is to weigh the positive aspects of using an existing product against the negative ones. As I mentioned previously, the most positive aspect is the training issue; by using an existing product, you cut down on the need to train your users and programmers to use a new interface or application. Training costs are usually a significant part of the personnel budget, so reducing the amount of training needed can represent substantial cost savings.

By using an existing application, you also have a means of combining the data stored in a server with data stored in another database or spreadsheet for reporting or analysis purposes. For example, the accountants in the finance department can query the database to get the latest inventory or sales figures, and then combine that data with other financial information stored in a local spreadsheet. The accountants can then use the spreadsheet application to analyze the combined data and create reports on the company's current fiscal status.

Most companies have a significant amount of critical data in an existing PC- or host-based DBMS (commonly referred to as a *legacy system*). By using an add-on, you can gradually migrate from the legacy system to the new C/S database without disrupting the day-to-day operations of the business.

Finally, it takes less programmer effort to use an existing product than it does to create a completely new application for accessing the database. The programmers can simply add the appropriate database access statements to the existing application, without having to rewrite the application from scratch. The users can continue to use the application as they did before; the only noticeable difference would be the new capabilities provided by the database server access.

The biggest negative is the extra overhead involved in accessing a database server from an application that isn't designed for that purpose. The overhead comes from two sources; first, the database link driver has to translate the data requests from the application's native language to the SQL the server understands before transmitting the query. Then the link driver has to take the data it receives in response to the query and reformat it into a form that the application can use. Because of this additional overhead, the database links for DOS-based applications usually require additional extended memory on the client system. This pretty much limits the client systems to those based on Intel 80286 or better CPUs.

The same is true for applications based on Windows 3.*x*. The add-on database drivers require the application to run in Windows's Standard mode and also need at least 1MB of RAM, which also requires an 80286 or better CPU. An application add-on may be the best excuse you'll ever have for retiring all those old XTs and upgrading all the ATs still hanging around your organization.

Finally, an application add-on may not give you the same complete access to the database server that a dedicated front end can. The limitations imposed by the translation steps may restrict the database operations to queries only. Or, the application may not support the exact same datatypes as the database server, requiring numerous translations between what the application can use and what the server can store. Some data elements may have to be modified or truncated before they can be stored on the server, leading to potential data losses or inaccuracies.

To sum it up, using an application add-on requires some compromises between capabilities and functionality. I don't recommend using an add-on as the only method for accessing data on a database server, or even as the primary method. An add-on, however, may represent the best choice for casual database users, or for those whose primary need is to query the database and combine the data retrieved with data stored in other applications. It can also serve as a short-term solution for providing database access until dedicated front ends are developed, and the data migrated from the application to the database server.

Paradox SQL Link

Borland's Paradox is well known for its user-friendly query-by-example (QBE) interface and semi-relational capabilities. Paradox's real strength is its QBE interface to SQL and SQL database servers, which makes it ideal for creating ad hoc queries. The Paradox SQL Link add-on module lets DOS Paradox users access data from a database server. SQL Link currently supports IBM OS/2 Database Manager and DB2 (through the MDI Database Gateway), Microsoft SQL Server, NetWare SQL, VAX Rdb/VMS, Borland's InterBase, and version 6.0 of ORACLE.

Features

SQL LINK for version 6.0 of ORACLE requires Paradox 4.0 for DOS and a 80286 or better workstation with a minimum of 2.5MB of RAM. In order to access data from the ORACLE server, you must first run a utility provided with SQL Link that creates a "replica" table on the client system. *Replica tables* translate the data between the server's format and Paradox. Once the replica is created, Paradox translates requests for data from the client into a SQL statement, and transmits this statement to the server. The response is sent back to Paradox and converted into a standard Paradox ANSWER table, using the replica table as a model. The ANSWER table can then be manipulated or saved locally, just like any other Paradox table.

Data translations are handled automatically; however, there are no Paradox equivalents for ORACLE's LONG and LONG RAW datatypes. If a queried column in ORACLE's database contains one of these datatypes, Paradox ignores the data and returns a blank column in the user's ANSWER table. There are also incompatibilities between Paradox's short integer (S) datatype and ORACLE's NUMBER datatype. Because of this, Paradox can't properly handle the translation for numbers between 32,768 and 99,999, so it returns a blank value.

SQL Link adds statements to the Paradox Application Language (PAL) that let the programmer access the database server through a custom application. It also adds the ability to send native SQL commands to the server from a PAL application; however, only one SQL command can be used at a time, and they can't be nested.

Supported Platforms

Paradox SQL Link supports only the DOS version of Paradox at this time. Paradox for Windows was released early in 1993, and a Windows version of SQL Link is due to be released in late 1993.

Superbase

Software Publishing Corp.'s (SPC) Superbase is a Windows 3.*x* DBMS that makes designing databases, forms, and reports a mostly point-and-shoot affair. It provides full support for DDE connections to other Windows applications. (DDE is an interprocess communication protocol supported by Windows and OS/2 that lets applications running on the same system dynamically share data.) The Superbase SQL Library is an optional module that links Superbase to XDB Systems' XDB-DBMS, Gupta's SQLBase Server, ORACLE, and Microsoft SQL Server.

Features

In addition to accessing its own database files and data from a server, Superbase can use dBASE III and dBASE IV data files for lookups and multifile reports on a read-only basis. It also supports its own type of BLOB data through an external-file field type, which lets the developer link a particular record to an external text file, or more importantly, to an external graphics file. The graphical images are displayed on the screen, along with the record they're attached to, making Superbase ideal for such applications as personnel identification or parts inventories.

Superbase's Database Management Language (DML, not to be confused with the SQL DML) is a superset of structured BASIC, with over 200 different commands. Superbase uses Windows to its best advantage; for example, the included Forms Designer module is a paint-type program that uses a tool-kit bar, pop-up selections, and point-and-drag capabilities to create query forms. A form can access multiple data sources; the links are created between various files through pop-up selection lists, and are displayed with graphics for checking and reference. Reports can also be designed through the Forms Designer or programmed directly in DML. Like DataEase (covered later in this chapter), Superbase's forms-based query-and-reporting features, and its ability to link multiple data sources into a single query, make it equally capable as a front end to a database server or as a data-integration tool.

In late 1992, SPC announced that it was discontinuing InfoAlliance, the company's high-end data integration, reporting, and analysis program, and that InfoAlliance's features would be rolled into the next version of Super-base. InfoAlliance was available in Windows and OS/2 versions, and used a proprietary C/S database as the basis for both its own data processing, and for links to other databases. Its main strengths were its easy-to-use reporting features, and its ability to create complex applications through a visual application-development module that freed the developer from writing any code. If SPC succeeds in integrating the best features of InfoAlliance, Super-base could potentially become the best database integration-and-reporting application for Windows users.

Supported Platforms

Superbase is a Windows 3.*x* product and doesn't support any other environments at this time. SPC has not formally announced an OS/2 2.0 or Windows NT version, though industry rumors state that the company is working on a new version of Superbase for one or both of these operating systems.

R:BASE for Vanguard

Microrim is the well-known vendor of the R:BASE series of relational data-bases for Intel chip–based PCs. From its earliest versions, R:BASE was the one PC-based database that most closely followed the relational model, and its built-in command language closely followed SQL standards. In the late 1980s, Microrim announced its ambitious Vanguard project, an attempt to create its own client/server database system.

Unfortunately, the company went through some difficult financial periods, and the Vanguard project was significantly scaled back. Microrim took the C/S technology it developed under the project and rolled it into the R:BASE for Vanguard (or R:BASE/V) line of products. Four versions of R:BASE/V are available, one each for connections to the Microsoft SQL Server, Ingres VMS, VAX Rdb/VMS, and ORACLE VMS.

Features

R:BASE/V is based on version 3.1c of R:BASE; it runs under DOS or OS/2 and requires at least 1MB of RAM. It's 100 percent compatible with applications created for the regular versions of R:BASE. The VAX/VMS version is the only ORACLE server supported at this time, though Microrim plans on expanding that support to other versions over the next several years.

R:BASE's best feature has always been its excellent application generator, which guides the developer through the process of creating the database, designing the database's forms and reports, and creating the user menus. When the process is complete, the generator creates and compiles the program's code. The application can be run as is, or the developer can customize the code and recompile it. Unfortunately, Microrim has not yet updated the R:BASE standalone program compiler to support version 3.1 applications. Applications created under R:BASE/V have to be run under the full environment, so each user must have a copy, or the company must have a multiuser license.

R:BASE's command language is compatible with the ANSI SQL Level 2 standard, so few translations are needed when using it to query data on the ORACLE server. R:BASE/V also lets the developer include PL/SQL statements in applications. Programs are written in plain ASCII text and compiled into a binary format for faster execution. R:BASE/V supports both the traditional R/> command-line prompt and the newer, menu-driven interface shown in Figure 5.1. The menu interface makes it easier for both programmers and non-programmers to create complete database applications from the ground up, including the database itself, the tables in the database, and any forms and reports needed.

Figure 5.1

R:BASE/V uses a menu-driven interface to guide the user or developer through database creations and accesses.

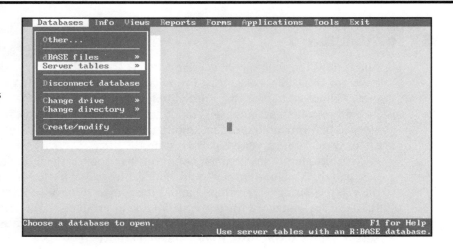

The most significant addition the menu interface brings to R:BASE is the QBE form, which makes it simple to create ad hoc queries on one or more tables in a database. The QBE screen is an enhancement to the earlier prompt-by-example interface that's still available through the R> prompt.

R:BASE/V for ORACLE continues to support an earlier implementation of the Vanguard technology found in all current R:BASE versions: the dBASE link. R:BASE can directly access dBASE-type files in their native format for both queries and updates, through the menus or from applications written in the command language. This lets users combine data from local dBASE applications with the data on a VAX server by using standard SQL commands.

Like Paradox SQL Link, R:BASE/V supports only ORACLE's CHAR, DATE, NUMBER, and VARCHAR datatypes. Unfortunately, this also means there is no direct correspondence between R:BASE's and ORACLE's character datatypes. The R:BASE TEXT field can store up to 1,500 characters, and the NOTE field up to 4,092 characters. Both types are much larger than the 255-character limit of ORACLE's CHAR and VARCHAR fields, and data may be truncated when moved from an R:BASE database to the ORACLE server.

Supported Platforms

R:BASE/V runs on systems using DOS 3.1 or later, or OS/2 1.1 or later. At this time, it can access only data from the VAX/VMS version of ORACLE. Because of this, the only supported network is version 4.0 of Digital's Pathworks, which uses the DECNet protocol.

The fact that R:BASE/V supports only ORACLE VMS is a severe limitation and keeps it from being more widely used. However, R:BASE/V could serve as the ideal front end for an organization looking to expand its VAX-based database into a C/S system. This is particularly true if you're looking for an easy way to integrate existing dBASE-type databases with a centralized database running on a VAX.

DataEase

DataEase International's DataEase is an easy to use but powerful PC-based DBMS that uses query forms as its primary user interface. DataEase SQL is a full DOS and OS/2 version of the basic DBMS that also provides access to ORACLE, Microsoft SQL Server, IBM OS/2 Database Manager, and IBM DB2 database servers, as well as to native DataEase files and applications.

In late 1992, the company released DataEase Express for Windows, a scaled-down version of the DBMS that runs under Windows 3.*x*. The initial release uses an ODBC driver to access dBASE, Microsoft SQL Server, and Sybase SQL Server databases; drivers for ORACLE, IBM Database Manager, and other database servers are planned for mid-1993 release. DataEase for Windows, a Windows-based version of the full DataEase DBMS, should also be released at that time.

Features

DataEase SQL transparently integrates database server access into the forms-based DataEase environment. For example, a user specifies the data source associated with a form only once—when the form is first created. From that point on, the links to the data are made without user intervention.

The secret behind this is a DataEase facility called PRISM: the Processing Router for Integrated SQL Management. PRISM converts the DataEase functions and DataEase Query Language (DQL) statements into optimized SQL statements, and transmits them to the database server. DQL's syntax is similar to SQL, and because it shares many of the same commands and functions, there isn't much overhead in the translation process. Application developers can also include native SQL statements in a DQL application.

DataEase SQL's forms-based environment makes it a capable data-manipulation, query, and reporting tool. It can simultaneously access multiple database sources from the same application, so it can also be used for integrating data from different database servers into the same application.

DataEase Express for Windows is mostly backward-compatible with the DOS and OS/2 versions, and can access databases and forms created by them. The reverse isn't true, however; the character-mode versions can't access forms and databases created under Windows. It also doesn't support the full DQL. This can be a problem for those looking for a single front-end application for their DOS and Windows users. It's possible that DataEase for Windows will solve these incompatibilities. However, any compatibility claims remain pure speculation until the product is actually released.

The DataEase SQL Connect drivers for ORACLE were not available at the time of this writing, so I'm unable to say if DataEase for Windows or DataEase Express for Windows will integrate into a C/S system as well as their character-mode counterparts.

Supported Platforms

Versions of DataEase SQL are available for DOS 3.1 or later, and OS/2 1.1 or later. These require at least an 80286-level PC with 2MB of RAM. DataEase Express for Windows has the same requirements, though the company recommends using Windows 3.1 with 4MB of RAM for best performance. DataEase for Windows' requirements will most likely be the same.

Q&A

Symantec Corp.'s Q&A is a flat-file database (or nonprogrammable database, as they're now commonly called) that's primarily designed for managing simple tasks, such as maintaining mailing lists or other small databases. Like most nonprogrammable databases, its primary interface is menu-driven, making database creation and manipulation easier. It is unique among the nonprogrammable databases because it has an add-on module that lets it query and report on data from either ORACLE or Gupta SQLBase servers; Symantec has promised support for other C/S databases in future releases.

Features

Figure 5.2 shows the streamlined menu interface that Q&A presents to the user. The Link-to-SQL module is available directly from Symantec by using the mail-in card included in the package.

Figure 5.2

Symantec's Q&A is the only nonprogrammable database currently available that lets the user access data from an ORACLE server.

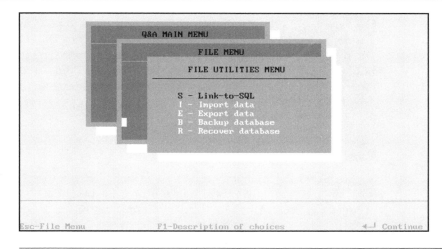

Q&A can also perform data lookups from external Q&A databases, or directly from dBASE III and dBASE IV data files, without having to import the data into the current database. Q&A has a complete built-in word processor that makes it easy to incorporate information from a database into letters and documents (this procedure is commonly referred to as a mail merge). It supports multiple printer fonts and has a built-in spell-checker and thesaurus, making it ideal for creating professional mail-merge letters.

Another of Q&A's unique features is its Intelligent Assistant, a natural-language interface to the database that lets the user enter queries in plain English. The Intelligent Assistant's query guide lets the user choose the data operators, the field names, and unique values for the fields from pop-up menus, greatly simplifying the process of creating an ad hoc query. Q&A is a great tool for users who have limited database needs but occasionally have to access a database server.

Supported Platforms

Q&A is available only for systems based on DOS 3.1 or later. The base-priced package can run on a standard 640K system; however, at least 1MB of additional expanded memory specification (EMS) RAM is required to run the Link-to-SQL module.

Lotus 1-2-3

There are also add-on modules that let spreadsheet users query data from a C/S database. Lotus Development Corp. has added this support to the DOS, Windows, and OS/2 versions of Lotus 1-2-3 through its DataLens drivers. DataLens drivers for SQL Server, dBASE, and Paradox are included with Lotus 1-2-3 for Windows, and are available for an additional cost for the other versions. Lotus has made it easy for other vendors to provide DataLens drivers for their own DBMSs, and Oracle sells a Lotus 1-2-3 DataLens driver for the ORACLE RDBMS.

Features

Spreadsheets are commonly used for analyzing, charting, and reporting on data, so they're an obvious choice for users who are already familiar with the product and need to analyze the data that resides on a database server. Database access is limited to queries only, as shown in Figure 5.3; the user connects to the appropriate driver and sends a SQL command to the database server to open the appropriate database.

The DataLens driver then translates the spreadsheet's data-import requests into SQL and sends them to the server. The server's response is translated into the spreadsheet's native format, and the user can then manipulate the query's results just like any other spreadsheet's.

Spreadsheets are particularly handy for analyzing data trends, through the built-in "what if?" functions that let the user project different results based on changes in one or more factors. By using a spreadsheet for "what if?" analysis of a database, the user can manipulate the data as much as he or she wants without affecting the real data still stored in the database server.

Figure 5.3

Lotus 1-2-3's DataLens driver lets the user connect to a remote database and create queries that are then returned in the native spreadsheet format.

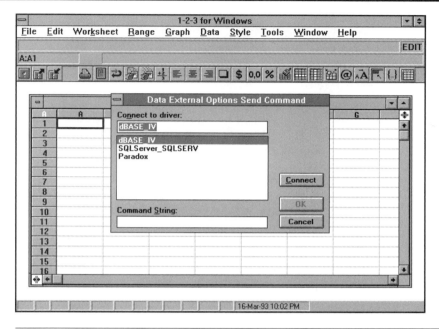

Lotus 1-2-3's built-in charting functions make it easy to create a number of different graphics based on the data extracted from the database. Users can use the data as the basis for line, bar, scatter, and pie charts (among others) to get a visual representation of the information being analyzed.

Supported Platforms

Lotus 1-2-3 comes in versions for DOS, Windows 3.x, and OS/2 1.2 or later. The Windows version includes DataLens drivers for dBASE and Paradox data files, and for connecting to a Microsoft SQL Server. DataLens drivers for the ORACLE RDBMS for all three versions are an extra-charge option available directly from Oracle.

Advanced Revelation

Revelation Technologies's Advanced Revelation is a PC-based database that's primarily aimed at database application developers. Advanced Revelation calls on its ability to incorporate optional modules that let users access data files from other database systems (including database servers), using the standard Advanced Revelation languages and the programming environment's environmental bonding. Environmental bonds for ASCII and dBASE III files are included in the product. Bonds for Microsoft SQL Server, ORACLE, Net-Ware SQL, and IBM DB2 are available from Revelation Technologies for an additional cost.

Features

Advanced Revelation is a sophisticated program-development environment. It uses a combination of pull-down menus, on-screen forms, and built-in editing tools to guide the programmer through the application design process. It includes four different programming languages: SQL, R/BASIC, R/LIST, and TCL. Each language has its own specialized function.

The built-in SQL is mostly used for accessing external databases. The primary language is R/BASIC, which has a wide range of functions for manipulating both the data and the Advanced Revelation environment. R/BASIC also includes a variety of debugging routines and tools.

Reports can either be designed directly through programming in R/LIST (the report-writer language), or through the EasyWriter report generator, which creates R/LIST routines from your design. TCL (The Command Language) is the master-control language for all of Advanced Revelation, and it combines a command-line language and a job-control language. TCL routines control the overall execution of applications by displaying windows and calling the appropriate R/BASIC and R/LIST modules.

The recently released Advanced Revelation 3.0 adds a query-by-example (QBE) screen to the program. The QBE screen makes it easy to query Advanced Revelation data, server data (through an environmental bond), or a combination of both. The QBE system automatically handles translating the queries into the appropriate R/BASIC or SQL code.

Supported Platforms

Advanced Revelation runs under DOS 3.1 or later, on an 80286 or better system. It requires at least 640K of RAM and will use EMS memory for better performance. Versions are also available for a number of Unix systems, including SCO Unix, HP-UX, Digital's ULTRIX, and IBM AIX. The Unix versions require at least 2.4MB of RAM and are source-code compatible with programs created with the DOS version.

Q&E Database Editor and Libraries

Pioneer Software's Q&E family of products provides a complete solution for integrating database access into Windows and OS/2 applications that otherwise have no means of accessing external database servers or files. The name

"Q&E" originally stood for "query and edit," but the various products' capabilities have been expanded beyond those simple functions, into full-fledged C/S front-end products. The Q&E products are so well-regarded that Microsoft licensed a version of the Database Editor to provide access to various SQL database servers from Excel.

In addition to ORACLE and both the Microsoft and Sybase versions of SQL Server, the Q&E products provide data access to a number of other database servers and files. Among the many external databases supported are Novell's BTrieve, NetWare SQL, dBASE-type .DBF files, IBM DB2, IBM OS/2 Database Manager, SQL/DS, SQL/400, Borland's Paradox, Microsoft Excel files, Ingres Server, Gupta's SQLBase Server, ASCII text files, and XDB Systems's XDB-DBMS.

Features

The flagship of the Pioneer line is Q&E Database Editor. Database Editor is a Windows- or OS/2-based graphical application that provides the user with data query and update capabilities. Users can either create customized forms for accessing and manipulating the data, or they can use Query Builder to create complex SQL statements. Figure 5.4 shows one of Query Builder's many dialog boxes. The Conditions screen uses drop-down pick lists to guide the user through the creation of the appropriate limiting portions of the SQL statement. When the whole statement is completed, the user simply clicks on an icon to send the statement to the appropriate database server or file. Queries can also be saved for future reuse.

Database Editor's real strength lies in its DDE capabilities. Users can create a DDE link between Database Editor and any other Windows or OS/2 application. Q&E then uses the DDE link to pass the results automatically from a query to the other application, where they are stored in the application's native format. This allows any application that supports DDE to access data from an external database server or file, regardless of whether the application itself supports such access.

The second product in the Q&E family is Database Library, which is a collection of DLLs for Windows or OS/2 that application developers and users can use to simplify the process of creating links to external databases from their application. The functions in Database Library can be called from any programming, script, or macro language supported by the application. Database Library's main advantage over Database Editor is its seamless integration with the user application. Users can directly access database files through the script or macro language they're familiar with, without having to load a separate program and create DDE links.

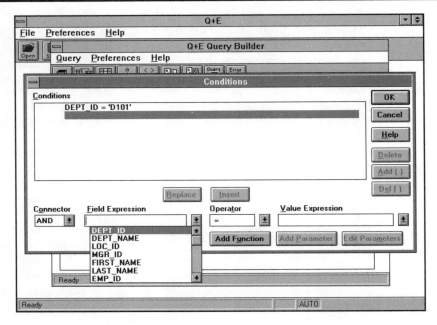

Figure 5.4
Pioneer Software's Q&E uses a series of dialog boxes and pick lists to guide the user through the process of creating complex SQL statements.

Database Library handles the appropriate translations between the native language and SQL. Actor, Ami Pro, BASIC, C, C++, Lotus Notes, Realizer, Smalltalk, ToolBook, and Microsoft Word for Windows are among the many applications and programming languages that can use Database Library.

The final two products are specialized versions of Database Library. Q&E DataLink/OV is designed specifically for use with Borland's ObjectVision application-development environment, and Q&E DataLink/VB for use with Microsoft Visual Basic. Both products provide access to all the database files and servers supported by Database Editor. They also share Database Library's advantage of seamless database access.

Supported Platforms

The Q&E Database Editor runs under Windows 3.*x* and OS/2 1.3 or later. Versions of Database Library and Q&E DataLink/OV are also available for both Windows and OS/2. Q&E DataLink/VB comes only in a Windows version, as there is no OS/2 version of Visual Basic at this time.

Miscellaneous Others

There are a few other products that provide links to ORACLE servers. These products have relatively small market shares and aren't in wide use; however, if you happen to use one of them, you will be glad to know that you can continue to do so while expanding its reach to the database server.

Clarion

Clarion Professional Developer, from Clarion Software Corp., is a PC-based database application-development package that has a small but loyal following. It uses add-on drivers to give application developers access to a wide variety of C/S DBMSs, including Microsoft SQL Server, XDB Systems's XDB-DBMS, Ingres, and ORACLE. Clarion has an IMAGE datatype that's similar to Superbase's external file datatype, which lets the programmer add graphical pictures to the database. Clarion is available only for DOS systems.

PC/Focus and PM/Focus

Information Builders Inc. (IBI) is best known as the vendor of Focus, a DBMS based on the network model that started out on minicomputers and was later ported to PCs. Rather than create its own C/S RDBMS, IBI is making its mark on the C/S market with EDA/SQL, the common SQL API that was discussed in Chapter 4. IBI has positioned its PC/Focus (DOS) and PM/Focus (OS/2) databases as environments for creating front-end applications for the database back ends supported by EDA/SQL, one of which is ORACLE, version 6.0. PC/Focus and PM/Focus almost cross the line into being pure application-development tools, but their continuing support for Focus databases keeps them in the add-on category for now.

Wingz

Informix Software is widely known as a RDBMS vendor; however, it also sells an interesting GUI-based spreadsheet application called Wingz. Wingz is unique in the spreadsheet market because versions are available for all the major GUI environments, including Windows 3.x, OS/2 2.0, Apple's System 7, NeXT's NeXTStep, and the Unix-based Motif and Open Look GUIs. Informix provides links to database servers through add-on modules called DataLinks. Informix sells a DataLink for its own INFORMIX-Online DBMS and NetWare SQL. Fusion Systems Group is a third-party vendor that provides other DataLink modules, which let Wingz access ORACLE and Microsoft SQL Server databases.

Query and
Reporting Tools

WHEN YOU'RE SETTING UP A C/S SYSTEM, YOU'LL FIND THAT NOT ALL of your users need full read and write access to the database. Some may only need to do queries to look up data already in the database. Or they may have to create weekly or monthly activity reports based on the data. Either way, there's no need for these users to have a full-featured front-end application that lets them add or update the data in the database.

Query and reporting front ends are ideal for this situation. These applications are usually geared toward providing read-only access to the database. They may let users create ad hoc queries and reports on the fly, or may only let the users run predefined queries and reports created by the application programmers or DBA.

The read-only access provided by query and reporting tools adds an extra level of security to your database as well. The security levels in the standard versions of ORACLE only let you control user access to the table level. But you may have data in a table that you don't want certain users to see; for example, you may not want some of the lower-level clerks in the personnel department to have access to the salary amounts of employees above a certain level. Queries and reports can be set up for such cases so that the users only have access to a limited portion of the data in the table. The queries and reports can be programmed to return only rows that meet the proper criteria, or only return certain columns in the table, giving you an extra measure of protection for confidential data.

Evaluating Query and Reporting Tools

There's one factor that's more important than all the others when you're evaluating a query and reporting front end for your organization: The software should be easy to use. The idea behind a query and reporting tool is that the software is designed for those who only need occasional or limited access to the database, so it should be simple for users to run the query or report. Applications that are hard to understand and use aren't used much.

From that point, you have to decide if you want your users to be able to create ad hoc queries and reports, or if you want them to run only prewritten queries and reports. Perhaps you want a combination of the two. In the latter two cases, you should make sure that the front end you're choosing has the ability to store the queries and reports on disk. It should also be simple for the user to run the stored query or report, either from a pick-list or from the front end's command line.

Of course, you'll also have to decide if you want a character-mode query and reporting tool, or one based on a GUI. For character mode, your choices are pretty limited; only R&R Report Writer for ORACLE, from Concentric Data Systems, supports character-mode applications under DOS and Unix.

All of the other tools in this chapter run under Windows or on a Macintosh. If you absolutely have to have character-mode front ends, you'll need to consider one of the front end add-ons discussed in Chapter 5.

Ease of use is a function of both the application's interface and its query capabilities. The interface has to be easy to understand, a feat usually accomplished through pull-down menus that guide the user through creating and/or running queries and reports. The user shouldn't have to know SQL to create a query; the front end should at the very least let the user pick and choose the desired columns and the conditions for the query or report from a dynamic list created on the fly from the actual contents of the database. This is where a front end based on a GUI shines, which can influence your decision of which products to investigate.

If you're going to use prewritten queries and reports, the built-in scripting language (these tools rarely have full programming languages) should be both powerful and flexible. Your application programmers shouldn't have to spend more than a few hours or at most a few days creating the queries and reports. The programmers should also be able to get to the script itself, through either a built-in or external editor, to do any necessary fine-tuning. The query and reporting tool should also have a way of tokenizing or encrypting the code behind the queries and reports, to prevent the users from making inadvertent changes.

Though I've lumped them all into the category of query and reporting tools, the available products are usually better at one function or the other. Some have excellent query capabilities but only minimal reporting features, and others are the opposite. Some do both equally well. You have to determine which function you have the greater need for before you can properly evaluate these products for use in your organization.

As with all the front end products I've covered to this point, you'll also have to decide if you need one that works with more than one DBMS. Most organizations have data in more than one format. A front end that lets the users create queries and reports from combinations of databases can go a long way toward solving the problem of integrating existing databases with a new C/S system.

The final point to keep in mind is the issue of licensing fees or runtime modules that I raised in Chapter 4. This is particularly true if you're planning on distributing prewritten queries and reports to your users. Be sure to factor in the additional costs of any licensing fees or runtime modules required, and compare them with the costs of having to buy more than one complete copy of a front end.

Quest

Gupta's Quest is the little brother to Gupta's SQLWindows, which I discussed in Chapter 4; it's available as a standalone program or as part of the SQLWindows Corporate Edition package. Quest is a Windows-based query and reporting tool that uses dialog boxes to insulate the user from the underlying SQL requests. It also has a number of built-in functions to assist in analyzing the data, and can be used as a tool to pass query results to other Windows programs for further analysis.

Like SQLWindows, the single-user basic package comes with a standalone version of SQLBase Server, which lets the user create and use a local database or access an existing SQLBase Server PC. It can also directly access dBASE-type and Paradox data files, so it can be used for some limited data integration. Support for ORACLE and other back-end databases is supplied through the various routers and gateways that Gupta sells.

Features

Quest's main feature is its easy-to-use interface. A series of dialog boxes, picklists, and drop-down menus leads the user through the process of choosing the database, tables, and columns to query, as shown in Figure 6.1.

Figure 6.1

Gupta's Quest lets you use a pop-up pick-list to choose the tables to be queried.

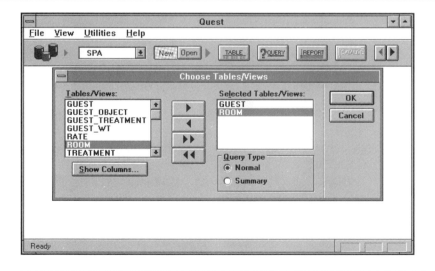

Other dialog boxes, lists, and menus let the user set the sort order and conditions for the query. Multitable joins are created through a dialog box that displays a graphical link between the columns the tables will join to. Figure 6.2 shows how Quest's built-in intelligence automatically displays a link between columns in different tables that have the same name. The user can either go with that link, add more links, or create a completely different one.

Figure 6.2

Quest automatically creates the query link between columns with the same name in two or more different tables.

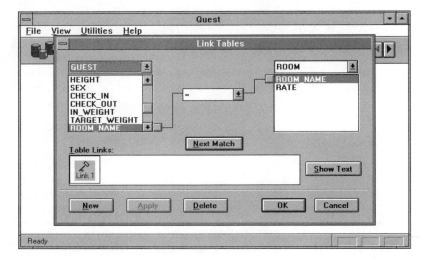

Quest also provides a dialog box-driven function editor, which has a large number of math, string, date, and time functions that create new columns in the result set for analyzing the data. A query can be saved for reuse or reports once the user is satisfied it's working properly. Quest can also use DDE to pass the query results to another Windows program for further analysis or charting. All of this can be done without the user knowing or using a single line of SQL.

Quest isn't strictly a query tool; users can modify the columns and data in local tables, create new tables, and import data into the local database from an external dBASE or Paradox file. By using the data returned from a query, Quest can also create local tables that the user can further manipulate without affecting the data stored on the server. These capabilities also give Quest the ability to serve as a standalone DBMS that can be expanded to a C/S system as your needs grow.

Reporting is another of Quest's strong features. It includes a full-screen report painter that uses dialog boxes to set the report size and format. Reports are based on existing saved queries or local database files, and can be previewed on the screen prior to printing.

A number of formatting options are provided, including adding graphical borders to fields, controlling blank lines, and printing different fields in different fonts. Bitmapped (.BMP) graphics such as a letterhead can be added to a report for viewing or printing.

In addition to the numerous query functions, Quest has a set of aggregate and nonaggregate functions that can be used in a report. The report functions let the user do data analysis on the components of the report through statistical functions such as minimums and maximums, sums, and data counts. They also provide numerous string functions for extracting portions of text fields, or converting fields between numeric and text formats. Quest's reporting functions also make it easy to create mailing labels or form letters that use the data in a database for the fill-in information.

Quest doesn't have a native programming or scripting language. It can be indirectly programmed through DDE links with Visual Basic programs, or through macro languages such as those in Microsoft Excel or Microsoft Word for Windows.

Quest's biggest limitation is that it doesn't directly support joins or views from multiple data sources, as it can only access one database at a time. The only way to create multidatabase joins is to query each database and save the results to a local database. Joins can then be done on the tables in the local database.

Supported Platforms

Quest is only available for Windows 3.*x*. You can buy it as a standalone package or as part of Gupta's SQLWindows Corporate Edition Package. It directly supports Gupta's SQLBase database server; a single-user version of SQLBase is included in the package. ORACLE, IBM DB2, IBM OS/2 Database Manager, Microsoft SQL Server, and Informix can be accessed through the appropriate Gupta SQLGateway or SQLRouter.

R&R Report Writer for ORACLE

Concentric Data Systems's R&R Report Writer started life as an improvement to dBASE's limited report-writing capabilities. It has since grown to an entire family of products that let users create highly customized reports from dBASE, Lotus 1-2-3, NetWare SQL, ORACLE, Paradox, Quattro Pro, Symphony, and XDB-DBMS. R&R Report Writer for ORACLE is a character-mode application that lets you create complex reports from data stored in NetWare SQL, ORACLE, and XDB-DBMS databases.

Features

R&R is strictly a report-writing tool. It can only do queries as the basis for a printed report, so it can't be used for prewritten or ad hoc lookups from a database. R&R is aimed at casual or nontechnical users, and it uses Lotus 1-2-3–style command menus to create the report template. The menus guide the user through the process of choosing the columns for the report and setting the conditions for the data.

Once the user chooses the data files or tables on which the report is to be based, R&R creates a default report that includes all the columns in the table. The user can then customize it through keyboard commands, or by using a mouse to change the column display widths, formats, or location.

Report templates are compiled by an internal compiler into binary format. This helps speed report execution, and it also lets the report developer distribute the report to other users in a format that can't be inadvertently modified.

Unfortunately, R&R doesn't support graphics, even in the Windows version, so you can't include things like company letterheads or charts in a report. However, it does have extensive font support for HP LaserJet and PostScript printers, so you can at least control how the report looks.

Supported Platforms

R&R Report Writer for ORACLE is available for DOS and various flavors of Unix. R&R Report Writer for Windows only supports dBASE-type files at the time this was written; Concentric is working on Windows versions of the other R&R products, and it expects to release R&R Report Writer for Windows for ORACLE later in 1993.

Impromptu

Impromptu is a relative newcomer to the C/S field; released in early 1992, it hasn't quite caught on yet as a query and reporting tool. Cognos Corp. is hoping that the August 1993 release of Impromptu 2.0 will change that. Impromptu 1.0 is available for both Windows 3.*x* and Macintosh platforms; version 2.0 will only be available for Windows 3.*x* for the near future. Version 2.0 will have native support for dBASE and Paradox files, and for directly accessing ORACLE and Microsoft/Sybase SQL Server. It will also include ODBC support for other servers as drivers become available.

Features

In the first release of Impromptu, the query and reporting functions were separated into two different programs. Users first had to create the query, save it, and then run the report writer to create a report on the query. Version 2.0 lets the user create the query and report simultaneously, significantly improving the process.

Impromptu bases its queries and reports on catalogs—its own representations of the tables and columns in a database. Its catalogs present a somewhat object-oriented view of the data, so the user doesn't have to be concerned with the actual structure of the database. Impromptu includes a snapshot function that keeps a local copy of the database's structure, so the user can create queries and reports off-line and then connect to the database to run them.

Version 2.0 includes full support for Windows 3.*x*, including DDE, OLE, drag-and-drop editing, and dynamic pick-lists. It has a number of built-in reporting and summary functions, including totals, subtotals, averages, and counts.

Supported Platforms

Impromptu 1.0 is available for Windows 3.*x* and Macintosh systems. Version 2.0 will initially be available only for Windows 3.*x*; it will have native support for dBASE and Paradox files, and connections to ORACLE and both the Microsoft and Sybase versions of SQL Server. Cognos also has gateways available for connections to Digital's VAX Rdb/VMS, Borland's InterBase, and HP's ALLBASE.

ClearAccess

ClearAccess, from ClearAccess Corp., is a Windows-based query tool that's also a data link between a back-end database and Microsoft Excel or Informix's Wingz. Its ad hoc query capabilities are very easy to use and can be stored for reuse through script recording. It only supports ORACLE servers directly; other servers can be accessed through EDA/SQL or DAL. SQL Server PCs can be accessed through Sybase's Open Client software. ClearAccess Corp. is working on a local database server called ClearBase, which will let ClearAccess act as a standalone DBMS. ClearAccess was shipping with a demonstration copy of ClearBase at the time of this writing.

Features

ClearAccess's main screen consists of five icons that give the user the choice of running a script, editing a script, connecting to a database, querying the database, and quitting the program. Pull-down menus offer similar choices, as well as starting and stopping the script recorder, and creating a predefined JOIN of data from different tables.

The Query window is the heart of ClearAccess. Once a connection is established to a database, the Query window presents pick-lists of all the accessible tables in the database; when a table is chosen, the columns in the table are displayed in a second pick-list window. Queries are built by clicking on the columns and dragging them to a window on the right side of the query screen. The conditions and sorting options for the query are then chosen and entered, and the query is run. Other query options let the user format the results, create joins, and edit the various conditions prior to running the query. ClearAccess doesn't provide any statistical or mathematical functions beyond those provided by the supported back ends.

The results can be returned either to the screen or to the Windows Clipboard. Screen results are shown in a separate window that can be scrolled or enlarged; the results can also be saved to a file in ASCII, SYLK, or .WKS format for importing into other applications. Users will be able to join results from different databases by storing the different results sets in a local ClearBase database (similar to Quest and its local copy of SQLBase), and creating a JOIN on the local tables. Or, the results can be sent directly to the Windows Clipboard, to be manually or automatically pasted into another Windows application.

ClearAccess's real power comes from its scripting capabilities. The script language has over 50 commands, and scripts can be created by recording an ad hoc query or by direct editing in a text editor. Existing scripts can be edited through the built-in editor and are run from the RUN button on the main menu. Simple debugging is supported through the ability to pause scripts during execution, or to watch the actual back-and-forth dialog between the script and the database server in a separate window. The script language also lets the developer prompt the user for values during script execution, which lets you create ad hoc queries and run them through scripts.

The included ClearLinks modules let ClearAccess act as a direct automatic query link for Excel, Wingz, and other Windows applications using DDE. Other Windows applications can be started and stopped by a ClearAccess script, which lets the developer completely automate the process of querying the database and moving the results directly to another application for reporting or analysis. Excel is supported directly through an included Excel add-in document that lets Excel macro sheets directly access and run ClearAccess scripts to query databases and return the results to a spreadsheet.

A similar facility is provided for Wingz. ClearLinks for other Windows applications are under development.

ClearAccess is best used as a linking application; its strength lies in its ability to automate database access and automatically pass the results to other Windows applications for further reporting or analysis.

Supported Platforms

ClearAccess is only available for Windows 3.*x*. It can directly access ORACLE and ClearBase databases, and can use DAL or EDA/SQL to connect to other databases. It also uses Sybase's Open Client to connect to Sybase SQL Server.

DataPivot and DataPrism

Brio Technology's DataPivot and DataPrism are designed to work together; DataPivot is a reporting tool, and DataPrism provides the query capabilities and database links. Both programs originated on the Macintosh. DataPivot for Windows and DataPrism for Windows were released in 1992.

DataPivot uses Apple's System 7 Subscribe feature (similar to the DDE links in Windows) or DataPrism to get the data it reports on. DataPivot for Windows uses DDE, and it can also directly access Excel and Lotus 1-2-3 spreadsheets, text files, and data received from DataPrism for Windows queries. Both versions of DataPrism support direct access to ORACLE databases, as well as databases that can be accessed by DAL or Sybase's Open Client.

Features

DataPivot and DataPivot for Windows include the common reporting functions, such as averages, counts, and totals. It also lets the user create custom formulas that can be included in the report. Its strong point is its ability to create multilevel cross-tabulation reports, giving the user a handy data analysis tool. It can automatically recalculate a report when the data the report is based on is updated.

DataPrism and DataPrism for Windows make it easy to create queries by taking full advantage of the GUI's drop-down menus, dialog boxes, and picklists. Queries can be edited and saved for future use. DataPrism can export the results of the query to external programs for further analysis through System 7's Publish feature on the Macintosh, and DDE in Windows.

Supported Platforms

DataPivot and DataPrism run on the Macintosh. DataPivot for Windows and DataPrism for Windows run on Windows 3.*x*. The Windows version of DataPivot can directly access Excel and Lotus 1-2-3 spreadsheets, as well as import data in text format. Both versions of DataPrism can connect to ORACLE database servers, and any servers accessible through DAL or Sybase's Open Client.

Personal Access

Spinnaker Software Corp.'s Personal Access is a Windows-based hypermedia-like application that extends the concept of card stacks to user-oriented database access. Users can create cards that access data from an ORACLE database, as well as from Microsoft SQL Server, Sybase SQL Server, DB2, BTrieve, dBASE-type .DBF files, and Paradox data files.

Features

Personal Access is actually an integrated front end to Spinnaker's PLUS, a hypermedia applications development and management engine that also comes in a script-compatible Macintosh version. PLUS is an object-oriented system that lets the user create stacks of cards, which contain data objects such as text fields, data fields, graphics, and control buttons. However, the combination of Personal Access and PLUS is very resource-intensive, requiring at least a 386 system with a minimum of 4MB of RAM.

A PLUS stack consists of one or more cards that contain the actual data queries (see Figure 6.3). Cards are created by placing various objects on either the foreground (present on only the visible card) or background (present on all cards in the same stack). A series of floating toolboxes makes designing and placing objects easy. By itself, PLUS can only access data directly entered into the card stack.

Personal Access extends PLUS's cards by providing access to external databases. Users can create queries through dialog boxes and pick-lists, and a single card can contain queries from multiple databases. Up to 500 databases can be accessed through a single card to create complex lookups and interrelationships, which means that Personal Access can also be used for data integration and analysis. The user isn't limited to working with only one type of back end or database file at a time; if a common field exists, stacks can simultaneously access data from different database formats.

Cards can be designed to show only one record at a time, or to display multiple records in a table format. When a link exists between two or more

Figure 6.3

Personal Access and PLUS use hypermedia-like card stacks to provide access to a variety of data sources.

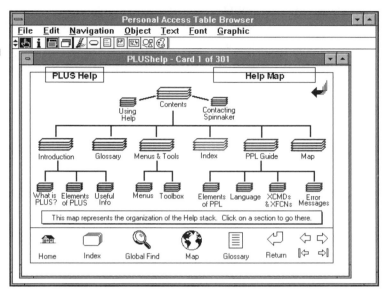

databases, later cards in a stack can contain other fields that are linked to the fields on the first card, giving the user the means to examine further the database's contents. For example, the first card can contain a query of all the departments in a company; when a particular department is highlighted, the second card in the stack can contain the results of a query of all employees in that department.

Designing database card stacks is easy, using the point-and-shoot toolkits. Personal Access and PLUS provide on-screen navigation menus that let the user move quickly around the stack. Floating toolboxes such as Quick Tools give the user easy access to the basic tools needed to create and browse card stacks, add fields to existing cards, or place predefined action buttons on the card. All the toolkits can be toggled on and off so they're not in the way when browsing data.

The PLUS Programming Language (PPL) is a event-driven scripting language that consists of over 200 command statements and functions that control Windows message handling, properties, navigation, visual and sound effects, menus, and other user-interaction tools. PPL scripts are automatically created when the cards are designed, and a built-in editor is included for more advanced customization of pre-created scripts, or for custom programming of card stacks.

PPL also provides support for DDE with other Windows applications, and can access external DLLs for more complete control over the Windows environment. When used with PLUS, Personal Access adds additional PPL commands to the language to support external database access.

PPL scripts can be used with any version of PLUS, making it easy to create applications for both IBM and Macintosh systems that access the same database servers.

External utilities that assist in database management are provided, and can be run directly from Windows or through Personal Access. The Table Maintenance utility lets the user create and change database files, and Joiner lets the user pre-create links between different database tables for later use in PLUS card stacks. Index Finder manages dBASE-type indexes, creating the associations needed for accessing .DBF files through Personal Access.

The included PLUS Reports module is a full-screen WYSIWYG report designer that lets the user create custom row-and-column or free-form reports, mail-merge letters, and forms from data contained in card stacks. Bit-mapped graphics from the clipboard can be included in reports, but only after they're copied to the clipboard from a card stack with a custom script. Reports can be printed or viewed in a window on the screen.

Also included in the package is PLUS View, which lets the user create dynamic row-and-column views of all the data contained in a particular stack. Views can be used as navigation tools or as a basis for quick summary reports based on a card stack.

Supported Platforms

Personal Access runs under Windows 3.*x*. PLUS is available for both Windows 3.*x* and the Macintosh. Personal Access can directly access data from Paradox and dBASE files, BTrieve, ORACLE, DB2, and SQL Server.

Oracle Card

Oracle sells Oracle Card, its own version of a hypermedia interface that uses the PLUS engine. Oracle Card is similar to Personal Access but can only access ORACLE databases. Many developers feel that Oracle Card isn't as powerful as the Personal Access/PLUS combination, and recommend using Personal Access instead of Oracle Card if you want to create hypermedia applications.

Features

Oracle Card's scripting language is an enhancement of PPL, called Oracle Talk, which lets users and developers issue PL/SQL and SQL commands from within a script. It creates new card stacks in one of two modes: standard or custom. If the user creates a standard stack, Oracle Card maintains all the database links and lets the user pick the appropriate tables and columns from pick-lists. Custom stacks require the developer to create manually all the appropriate links between the tables and columns in the database.

Oracle Card lets users add graphics to each card by storing bitmaps in LONG RAW data columns. The graphics are automatically displayed on the card when the data is queried. Due to the limitations of ORACLE 6.0, bitmaps can't be any larger than 64K.

Version 2.0 is due for release sometime in 1993 and will add more functions to the current product, including support for Microsoft's Pen Computing operating system. Version 3.0 will add support for Unix GUIs; it's scheduled for release in late 1993 or early 1994.

Supported Platforms

Oracle Card runs under Windows 3.x and on the Macintosh. It only connects to ORACLE databases, either local or on a server.

CHAPTER

7

Data Analysis Tools

I F YOU'RE ONLY USING YOUR DATABASE AS A PLACE TO STORE INFORMATION for lookups and reports, you're not using it to its full potential. The data holds a wealth of information about the past, present, and future state of your organization's business. The trick lies in unlocking that information so you can use it as one of the factors in making day-to-day business decisions.

The key to unlocking the information is a data analysis tool. Data analysis tools share many of the same features as the query and reporting tools discussed in the previous chapter. However, they go beyond these simple query tools by letting executives and managers examine more than just the current state of the data in the database. Analysis tools let you monitor the data for historical trends so that you can make decisions; for example, you can monitor the fluctuations in inventory levels, and use the information as the basis for decisions on increasing or decreasing the production of a particular item.

Analysis tools usually have charting capabilities built-in, so you can create graphical representations of the data you're monitoring. They may also provide you with a way of playing "what if," so that you can see the effect that changes in particular data items would have on the whole database, without affecting or changing the stored data. And finally, the high-end analysis tools let you combine information from multiple sources, such as other databases or spreadsheets, so that you can get a better picture of the current status of the entire organization. For this reason, they're sometimes referred to as data integration and analysis tools.

The most common form of analysis application is usually referred to as an *Executive Information System* (EIS). EIS applications are designed to gather data from a number of different places in an organization, and present the information in such a way that the organization's managers can use the information to make complex business decisions. For example, an EIS might combine data from the inventory, sales order, and personnel databases so that the manager can create vacation schedules that have a minimum impact on how fast orders are filled. Another name for EIS in common use today is a Decision Support System or DSS.

Integration and analysis applications can also be used for statistical or scientific studies, analyzing stock-market trends, or any place where the user needs to combine and examine data from multiple sources.

The proliferation of information in our modern businesses (and even our society) makes it very difficult to separate the important data from the stuff that's considered (for lack of a better term) "background noise." If you're going to invest your organization's time and money in creating and using a C/S system, you should definitely take the final step and include a data analysis tool as part of the package. That way, you're sure of getting the most value out of the data being stored. Along the way, you may discover that the data analysis tool becomes the most useful computer application you have.

Evaluating Data Analysis Tools

The most important factor when choosing a data analysis tool is that it support a wide variety of data sources. As I mentioned in the introduction to this chapter, the majority of analysis tools are used for EIS systems, where data is combined from multiple sources. To be really useful, an analysis tool should give you the ability to combine data from your ORACLE database with data stored in other databases (both traditional and C/S), as well as spreadsheets. Of course, the analysis tool should be able to access data from the other applications already in use in your organization. It should also let you add some type of drivers for additional data sources, so your EIS applications can grow with your needs.

Many of the tools I've discussed up to now already have some of these features. Before you spend your time and money investigating analysis tools, take a realistic look at your analysis needs. You might find that the application development toolkits or front-end applications already in use in your organization have all the features you need to create sophisticated analysis applications. If you find that these tools don't do everything you need, you can proceed with your evaluation of data analysis tools, confident that you won't be wasting money on software that duplicates the capabilities you already have in-house.

Analysis tools should share one important factor with query and reporting tools: They should be have an easy-to-use interface for end users. Most analysis tools are GUI-based, so this isn't as big of a problem as it might seem. The end user shouldn't have to do much more than pick a particular analysis task from a menu. However, an analysis application usually has a lot more going on than just performing a simple query on a database. The extra complexity involved in creating meaningful analysis queries and reports usually implies a more sophisticated understanding of the architecture behind the data sources. While some analysis applications can be created by the end user, the vast majority require some custom programming to make the best use of their power and features.

The next thing to look for is a sophisticated programming or script language that your application developers can use to create the analysis applications. That way, the difficult and complex data queries and combinations can take place "under the hood," without making the whole application too difficult to use.

The current trend in data analysis tools is to move away from requiring custom programming, and to move toward more intelligent design tools that let the programmer create complex applications thorough a point-and-shoot interface. The analysis tool itself combines the specified actions into the final program. This is where GUI-based analysis tools shine; the application

developer simply uses the tool bars, drop-down menus, and pick lists to define the data sources and create the appropriate queries for analysis.

The same built-in tools can be used to create the graphs, charts, and reports that the end user needs to analyze the data successfully. These actions are then combined by the analysis tool and stored in a command file that the end users can run to do the actual analysis. Either way, you should factor in the additional costs for application development personnel when you're figuring out how much an analysis tool will cost.

Data analysis tools have been around for quite some time, and many predate the C/S architecture. Because of this, you'll find that many of them support multiple platforms, so your choices aren't as limited as they are with query and reporting tools if you haven't made the commitment to a GUI yet. With the exception of Approach for Windows and LightShip, all the analysis tools in this chapter come in different versions for different platforms, and may even be available in GUI and character-mode versions.

Again, another point to keep in mind is distribution license fees or run-time modules, which can significantly increase the cost of the tool. On the other hand, most organizations that use analysis tools limit them to management personnel, and don't need as many copies as they would of a more general query and reporting tool. Be sure to factor the number of copies you need into your evaluations.

Forest & Trees

Forest & Trees, from Trinzic Corp., may be the easiest to use, yet it is the most powerful data analysis tool available for both DOS and Windows today. Forest & Trees was originally produced by Channel Computing, but Channel was purchased by Trinzic early in 1993.

The standard version lets the user combine data from most common PC file formats, including dBASE, Lotus 1-2-3, Microsoft Excel, Q&A, R:BASE and Paradox. The C/S version adds the capability to integrate data from a number of back ends besides ORACLE, including Microsoft SQL Server, Gupta's SQLBase, NetWare SQL, DB2 (through Micro Decisionware's Database Gateway), and Digital's Rdb/VMS. Its biggest limitation is that it's an analysis-only tool that accesses the data sources in read-only mode.

Features

As its name implies, Forest & Trees uses a tree-like structure to collect data from various sources into data objects on the screen. Each object is a node in the tree diagram, and can contain the results of a query on a particular data source, as shown in Figure 7.1. The objects can then be connected to other objects, creating higher-level nodes based on formulas that analyze and combine the data from lower-level nodes. All the nodes ultimately connect to a top-level (root) node that contains the complete analysis of the subnodes. Forest & Trees doesn't have a programming or scripting language, so all data access and analysis is done through objects, pick lists, and dialog boxes.

Figure 7.1

Forest & Trees uses a tree-like structure to collect and combine data for analysis from a wide variety of sources. Shown here are two different views of the interconnections between the different data elements.

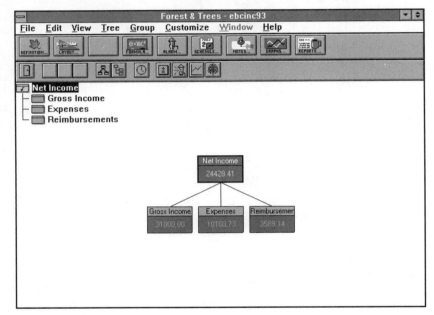

The easiest way to describe how Forest & Trees presents complex data for analysis is by an example. Suppose a business owner wants to look at the business's cash flow. The first step is to create objects that perform the queries to show the different parts of the cash flow, such as the income received, outstanding invoices, inventory, taxes paid, expenses, cash on hand, and investments. Each particular analysis node is created from a query on one data source for the item being examined; for example, the data for income can come from a set of Microsoft Excel spreadsheets, while the inventory data comes from an ORACLE database. Figure 7.2 shows the Forest & Trees data access screen, where the user specifies the data source for a particular node.

Once the lower-level nodes are created, the user then creates the second-level nodes that combine the results of the lower nodes into one node for income, and one for money spent. Finally, a top node is created, which subtracts expenses from income to show the company's profits.

Figure 7.2

Forest & Trees uses a common dialog box to access different data sources. It automatically recognizes the data source, based on the file or server type.

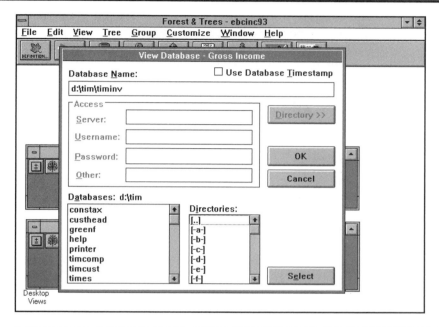

Forest & Trees presents all the nodes either as individual data objects, or as a tree with connecting lines showing which lower-level nodes make up which higher-level nodes. Navigating around the tree is easy; each node's display object has button icons that let you navigate up and down the tree to examine the data elements that compose the node. Other buttons let the user create a graph or report on the data the object represents; the user can even add pop-up notes to each node to indicate the meaning of the data, the assumptions behind the data query or calculation, or particular changes to watch for.

Forest & Trees's real power as an analysis tool comes from its ability to provide real-time data results, which let the user examine the data as it changes. This ability comes from the software's scheduling tool, which lets the application builder create a schedule for when the data in an object is updated. Automatic updating can take place after a set amount of time, such as once a day, once a week, monthly, yearly, or after a user-defined period of days, weeks, or months. If the application isn't running during a scheduled time, the updates are automatically performed the next time it's loaded.

Forest & Trees can also automatically save a history log of previous results from updates, which lets the user view and analyze the changes in a particular data object over a period of time. This feature is very handy for examining historical trends.

Along with scheduling, Forest & Trees lets the user set alarms for particular data conditions in each node. Alarms are indicated by color-coding the data displays in each object. Green means the data is okay, yellow means the data is approaching a cautionary level, and red means the data has triggered the alarm. Pop-up notes can be attached to the alarm to provide further information on what the alarm indicates. Again using our example, an alarm can be set for when expenses exceed 25 percent of total income, bringing the problem to the user's attention by turning the expense value red and popping up the alarm note.

Supported Platforms

Forest & Trees is available for both DOS and Windows 3.*x.* The standard edition supports accessing data from most common Intel-based PC file formats, including dBASE, Lotus 1-2-3, Microsoft Excel, Q&A, R:BASE, and Paradox. The C/S version extends the package's data access capabilities to ORACLE, Microsoft SQL Server, Gupta's SQLBase, NetWare SQL, DB2 (through Micro Decisionware's Database Gateway), and Digital's Rdb/VMS.

LightShip and Command Center

Pilot Software has two applications that qualify as data analysis tools. Light-Ship is a Windows-based data analysis package that's primarily designed for use by application developers to create EIS applications. The base-priced package uses DDE as the source for its data, and the optional LightShip Lens module lets LightShip access data from other PC-based databases, such as dBASE, Microsoft Excel, and Paradox. LightShip Lens modules are also available for ORACLE, Microsoft SQL Server, and NetWare SQL. Though it allows the user to update the data in the source files, its primary function is to provide the user with different views of the data for analysis.

Command Center is Pilot's high-end EIS development software. It's primarily designed for use on host-based Unix systems, VAX systems and mainframes, though MS-DOS, Windows 3.*x,* and Macintosh versions are available. Command Center can be used in a C/S system through the add-on Command Center SQL module, which provides access to ORACLE, IBM DB2, and SQL/DS, Rdb/VMS, Ingres, and Sybase SQL Server databases. Of the two, LightShip is the product that most users will want to use, so it will be the primary focus of the rest of this section.

Features

LightShip is object-oriented and uses a number of tools to create the different screen and data objects. The tools can either be accessed from the menu or from a floating-icon toolbar. LightShip refers to data objects as documents and can place them anywhere on the screen. Each document can display data from only one source; the only way to combine and compare data from different sources is by creating an object for each source on the screen, and manually comparing them.

The standard LightShip version uses either directly entered data, a text file, or a Windows DDE link as the source for a document, making it somewhat limited as an analysis tool, particularly if you've not yet moved your databases to Windows. The additional LightShip Lens module is needed to access LightShip's full power; once it's added to the system, the module is automatically available and invoked as a data source when a new document object is created. Queries are easily created through a series of pop-up windows and pick-lists that let the user or developer specify the data source, fields, and query conditions.

LightShip also has Hotspot objects, a facility that ties one or more actions to a particular object or to an item in a document. When used in a document, a Hotspot lets the application developer create a pick-list of items that the user can click on. The user can then view the document associated with that item in a separate object window on the screen.

One of LightShip's greatest strengths is its integration of screen displays and graphical image objects with data, which Figure 7.3 demonstrates. Clipboard, .PCX, and .BMP images can be added to a screen as screen backgrounds to highlight different documents in different areas of the screen. A graphical object can also be used as a Hotspot indicator; clicking on the graphic brings up other screens that contain documents associated with the particular data being analyzed. LightShip also gives the developer complete control over the screen palette for each object, which lets the developer highlight particular documents or portions of documents. This is particularly useful for creating data thresholds, where the color of an object can automatically change to reflect its value or status when it exceeds a programmer-defined limit. Data thresholds are similar to, though not as sophisticated and flexible as, the alarms in Forest & Trees.

LightShip is primarily an application-building tool. While novices can use it to query different data sources, building a complete analysis system isn't a simple process. LightShip is aimed at applications developers looking to create a simple-to-use EIS for their clients or upper management. It supports these capabilities by letting the developer create custom menus and screens with Hotspots that shield the user from the underlying program.

Figure 7.3

LightShip uses Windows's graphics capabilities to the fullest; it lets the developer mix both text and graphics on the same screen.

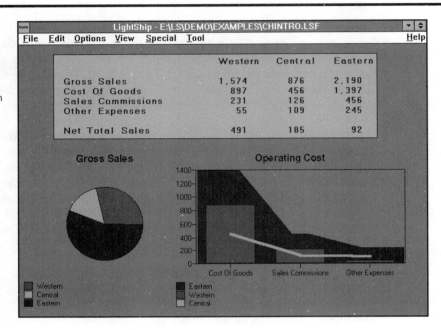

LightShip also includes debug facilities that let the developer test-run the application and watch the values of defined variables and the actions being executed through a trace. Debug traces can be saved on disk or printed out to make it easier to correct problems or errors. The debug facility also gives the developer information on any image objects being used.

LightShip's biggest drawback is that it has no easy way to create analysis links or show the relationship between different data documents. The only way to analyze data is by showing different documents on the same screen, and manually analyzing what's being shown; data from different documents can't be joined into composite views or results. Users also report that it's relatively slow compared to other products.

Command Center comes in both character-mode and GUI versions. It doesn't include LightShip's ability to add graphics to the screen, as it's more oriented toward use on terminals. Its built-in database support is limited; the Command Center SQL module is needed to access SQL-based RDBMSs. Command Center is better suited for creating EIS applications on host-based systems; those who are building a mixed host-based and C/S system can use Command Center to create the EIS system for terminal users, and LightShip for the networked C/S clients.

Supported Platforms

LightShip is only available for Windows 3.*x*. The base-priced package only supports data that's directly entered, or accessed through a text file or Windows DDE link. The optional LightShip Lens modules extend its data analysis capabilities to dBASE, Microsoft Excel, and Paradox files, as well as ORACLE, Microsoft SQL Server, and NetWare SQL database servers.

Command Center is available for VAX/VMS, IBM's MVS and VM mainframe operating systems, and numerous versions of Unix. Versions are also available for Intel-based PCs running DOS or Windows 3.*x,* and Macintosh systems. The Command Center SQL module is needed to access data stored in ORACLE, Ingres, IBM DB2, SQL/DS, Digital Rdb/VMS, and Sybase SQL Server databases.

GQL

Andyne Computing's GQL (for Graphic Query Language) is a combination query, reporting, and analysis tool for GUI systems. Though it has query and reporting functions, I've put it in the data analysis category, based on its special features aimed at EIS application developers. GQL is available for the Macintosh, Windows 3.*x,* and various Unix GUIs. It can access data from ORACLE, Rdb/VMS, IBM's DB2, SQL/DS, AS/400, Ingres, Sybase SQL Server, Informix, and Teradata databases. The Macintosh version can access any database that uses the Apple DAL protocol.

Features

GQL makes heavy use of the point-and-click capabilities of the underlying GUI. Application developers can use pick-lists, drag-and-drop objects, and dialog boxes to create complex queries. The queries can then be used as the basis for reports or data analysis. Queries can be written in GQL's built-in SQL (GQL automatically does the appropriate translations for different databases) and saved for reuse. Saved queries are interchangeable between the different platforms, so GQL can be used in organizations that have different platforms to support. Users can also use the built-in SQL features to create ad hoc queries.

GQL includes two features similar to LightShip: support for graphics in the on-screen forms, and Executive Buttons, GQL's name for on-screen action spots similar to LightShip's Hotspots. GQL's Executive Buttons can be icons, text, or on-screen graphics. Queries and reports can be associated with the Executive Button, and are automatically executed when the user clicks on it. Executive Buttons can also be associated with other GQL forms, providing the user with an easy way to move back and forth between different analysis screens.

GQL's data analysis features include the ability to create dynamic joins from tables in different databases. It uses the GUI's graphics to show the database links on the screen. The Windows version can automatically launch other Windows applications, such as Microsoft Excel and Microsoft Word, and pass data to those applications for more detailed analysis.

GQL provides its own security features that work in addition to those found in the underlying database. The built-in security features let the DBA tailor GQL's queries, reports, and analysis features for each individual user.

Supported Platforms

GQL is available for Windows 3.*x*, Macintosh, and Unix systems running Motif or Open Look. The Windows and Unix versions can access data from ORACLE, Rdb/VMS, IBM's DB2, SQL/DS, AS/400, Ingres, Sybase SQL Server, Informix, and Teradata databases. The Macintosh version uses Apple's DAL protocol to access ORACLE databases, or any others that can use DAL.

Approach for Windows

Approach for Windows is a relative newcomer to the Windows database arena. It's a full-fledged non-programmable database product in its own right, one that also provides data access and integration for a number of external databases. Approach can use either dBASE or Paradox files as its native format, though it uses its own indexing scheme. Its included PowerKey technology provides links to ORACLE, Microsoft SQL Server, and IBM DB2 databases.

Approach Software Corp. was founded by former developers from Claris (which sells the Macintosh and Windows-based FileMaker nonprogrammable database) and Oracle, and their software package reflects many of the best features of both technologies. Its data integration capabilities put it in this category, rather than the front-end add-ons covered in Chapter 5.

Features

Approach for Windows has an application design and development environment that's entirely visual and aimed at non-technical users. Users and developers create forms, queries, and reports through its point-and-shoot, drag-and-drop interface. Though it doesn't have a built-in script language (it does include a macro facility), advanced users and programmers can create text files containing SQL SELECT statements that can be executed from within the software as part of a query or report.

Approach for Windows can simultaneously access up to ten different database files from the various data sources it supports. Approach Software calls its proprietary data-access capability PowerKey. Figure 7.4 shows how Approach for Windows uses the Windows drop-down menus to pick from the various database formats it supports.

Figure 7.4

Approach for Windows can access up to ten different database files or tables at the same time; it supports dBASE and Paradox files as its native format, and can access data from ORACLE, Microsoft SQL Server, and DB2 databases.

Queries can be saved in .QRY files, and multitable/multifile views can be saved in .VEW files for later use. Approach extends the capabilities of the underlying databases by providing its own built-in support for storing graphics images with a database. Graphics can include .PCX, TIFF, .EPS, .BMP, and .WPM formats.

In addition to providing access to different file formats, Approach for Windows can translate data from one format to another. It can be used to move data from a dBASE or Paradox file to one of the database servers it supports, and vice versa.

It also provides full support for Windows 3.1's OLE capabilities. You can use OLE to embed other objects, such as a spreadsheet or word processing document, inside an Approach for Windows form or report. It includes over

80 math, string, date, and financial functions that can be included in a form or report for additional data analysis.

The software is actually a hybrid application. It can function as a stand-alone database, as a query and reporting tool, or as a full-fledged data integration and analysis tool. It doesn't have the sophisticated analysis features of the other applications in this chapter; however, its data integration features give the average nontechnical user the ability to start with a local database and grow the application into a functional data analysis system as the user becomes more familiar with the features and capabilities.

Supported Platforms

Approach for Windows runs on any Windows 3.x system. It uses dBASE or Paradox data files as its native format, with its own indexing scheme. The PowerKey technology lets it access data from ORACLE, Microsoft SQL Server, and IBM DB2 databases.

Intelligent Query (IQ) Access

IQ Software Corp.'s Intelligent Query (IQ) software is another multiplatform query and reporting tool designed for both the nontechnical end user and the application developer. Its data analysis features come from its capability to combine information from multiple data sources, and to format its reports for automatic use by external word processing and spreadsheet software. Versions are available for MS-DOS, Windows 3.x, OS/2, various versions of Unix, and Digital's VAX/VMS. IQ can access data from over 60 different DBMSs, including dBASE, ORACLE, Informix, Ingres, Microsoft SQL Server, Sybase SQL Server, Digital's Rdb/VMS, and all of IBM's RDBMSs.

Features

Though it's character-mode–based, IQ uses its own graphics capabilities to make it easy for the user to create complex queries and reports. It uses pull-down menus and pop-up windows to guide the user through the process of creating the query. Users create forms and reports directly on the screen through the built-in forms and reports painter.

Its reporting capabilities include cross-tabulation reports and over 30 standard mailing-label formats. Reports can be created from multiple data sources. Reports can be automatically formatted for importation into Word-Perfect and Microsoft Word documents, or Microsoft Excel and Lotus 1-2-3 spreadsheets.

IQ started out as a report writer for vertical-market–application programmers, and it still retains some of its early features. Queries and reports created in IQ can be called from other application development tools, such as Oracle's SQL*Forms and SQL*Menu, as well as programs written in 3GLs such as C and COBOL.

Supported Platforms

Intelligent Query is available for MS-DOS, OS/2, Digital's VAX/VMS, and various versions of Unix, including Digital's ULTRIX, IBM's AIX, and SCO XENIX.

A Brief Note about InfoAlliance and Superbase

In my first book, I talked about Software Publishing Corporation's (SPC) InfoAlliance, one of the first database integration and analysis applications. Unfortunately, SPC discontinued InfoAlliance shortly after the book was published, due to poor sales. However, SPC has announced that it will include some or all of InfoAlliance's data analysis capabilities into future versions of the company's Superbase DBMS (covered in Chapter 5). When that happens, Superbase may take InfoAlliance's place among the other analysis tools.

8

Miscellaneous Other Front Ends

Evaluating Specialized
and Other Front Ends

Expert Systems

CASE/Design Tools

Communications

Document and
Image/Graphics
Management

THERE'S AN OLD COMPUTER-INDUSTRY SAYING THAT GOES UNDER MANY names; I've usually heard it called the "80 percent rule." It states that the users of a product use 80 percent of the product's features 80 percent of the time. This "rule" can be restated to apply to the products themselves, meaning that 80 percent of users use the top 80 percent of products currently on the market.

The previous four chapters covered those products that generally make up the top 80 percent of the front-end market. The remaining 20 percent consists of the more specialized products and can be divided into two broad categories: miscellaneous other front ends and very specialized vertical market applications.

In this chapter I'll be covering the first of these two remaining categories; vertical market applications are discussed in Chapter 9. The miscellaneous-other category covers front-end products that fill a particular need or can be used to develop applications for a specific purpose. The information given in this chapter (and the next) won't be as detailed as it has been up to now; I'm including it primarily to give you an idea of what's available for some specialized needs you may have. You might find that an application you had planned to develop in-house is already available, which can save considerable programmer time and costs. If one of these products looks like it may do the trick, you can contact the vendor for further information. You'll find the contact information in Appendix B.

Evaluating Specialized and Other Front Ends

Deciding if one of these front ends or toolkits is right for your needs is rather simple. If you need an application that uses the services these front ends provide, and you don't want to have to develop it in-house or don't have the necessary expertise to do so, look into one of these products. Some are more like application development toolkits for specialized applications, but the previous statement still holds; if you don't want to spend the time designing your own application from the ground up, check out one of these specialized toolkits.

If the product runs on one or more of the platforms your organization uses, contact the vendor and discuss your specific needs. If the product is a close fit, the company will be more than happy to give you whatever information you need to make an informed purchase decision.

Even if a product isn't as close a fit as you need, don't give up. Many of these vendors will provide a customized version tailored to your particular organization. These products usually aren't shrink-wrapped packages that you can buy at your local computer store. The companies that sell them usually provide installation and configuration support, as well as extensive support after the product is up and running. Of course, this level of service doesn't come cheap, so expect to pay more up front for the product itself, and for the continuing support.

As with any other critical system, make sure that the vendor provides the support level that you need. If the software will be used 24 hours a day, seven days a week, check if the vendor provides that type of support. Also check on how the vendor provides updates and bug fixes; are they included as part of the support plan, or do they cost extra?

VARs

When you're dealing with a specialized product, you'll probably encounter a type of vendor different from the big software houses. Some of the products in this chapter and virtually all of the products mentioned in Chapter 9 are sold by VARs. A VAR goes beyond just selling you the software; VARs usually sell a complete solution, including some or all of the necessary hardware and the different software pieces you'll need. In addition to the front-end application, the VAR can also sell you the ORACLE Server software, perhaps a PC or Unix system to run it on, and the network cards, cables, and gateways necessary to have the systems talk to each other.

There's one caveat I would be remiss in not mentioning: Though the vast majority of VARs are reliable, knowledgeable companies that have been in business a while, they tend to be small outfits that consist of only a few employees. The VAR may even consist of a single person, such as a programmer who struck out on his or her own to develop and sell applications. Because the computer industry changes so rapidly and is so dependent on the general economy, a VAR that's a viable, profit-making operation today may go out of business next year. If the application you're purchasing from the VAR is mission-critical to your organization, you should also ensure that the source code is available to you should the VAR go out of business. That way, you can get the code and either maintain and update the application yourself, or hire a consultant to come in and do it for you. Note that this is also true if you hire a consultant to come in and design an application for you.

There are a couple of ways to handle the source-code issue. The easiest is to have the VAR provide it with the products. Most VARs are reluctant to do this, however, because their livelihoods are dependent on that code; they don't want their competitors to see how they've solved a particular problem, or any other secrets they may have in the code. A more reasonable compromise is to have the VAR store a current copy of the source code in a neutral place, such as a bank safety deposit box, and specify in your contract with the VAR that the code will be released to you should the VAR go out of business. The stored copy should be in both printed form and in the appropriate electronic format, such as a floppy disk or nine-track tape. If you do it this way,

make sure that your contract also specifies that the VAR will update the stored copy whenever it updates the copy in use at your company.

If you're looking for alternatives to the products discussed here, or for a specialized ORACLE application that's not covered, contact Oracle Corp.'s marketing department for a copy of its *Business Alliance Program Products and Services Catalog.* This catalog lists all the software vendors, VARs, system integrators, and consultants that provide ORACLE front ends, and also applications and support that the corporation knows about. The catalog is updated at least once a year, so the information it contains is relatively current.

Expert Systems

An expert system is a somewhat nebulous term that describes a class of applications designed to assist the user in the decision-making process. A more accurate term would be decision-support system, but expert systems have been associated with the long quest to create artificial intelligence (AI) in computer systems, so the term stuck. The line between an expert system and the analysis tools discussed in Chapter 7 can be very fuzzy at times; in some cases, the only difference is that the vendor calls its product an expert system for marketing purposes. However, the proper definition of an expert system is that it includes business rules for analyzing a particular business or scientific situation.

Expert systems have many wide and varied uses. One example of an expert system is an advanced analysis application that helps a business executive decide when and where to open a new store, factory, or office. Another example is a system that technical support personnel can use to look up solutions to common problems.

An expert system is usually custom-designed for the business that's going to be using it. While you can create your own from the ground up by using one or more of the tools described in previous chapters, you may find it easier to use one of the specialized expert-system design toolkits described in this section.

EXSYS Professional

EXSYS Professional by EXSYS is an expert-system design package that's aimed at everyone, from casual users with no programming experience to knowledgeable system engineers. Most users will need only a small portion of the command language to create a fairly complex expert system. Programmers can use the full command language to create complete turnkey systems that support a wide variety of decision-making processes. EXSYS closely resembles an analysis tool, and the only reason I've mentioned it here is because the vendor prefers to market it as an expert system.

EXSYS is available in both character-mode and GUI versions. Character-mode versions are available for MS-DOS, VAX/VMS, and many Unix variants. GUI versions are available for Windows, OS/2, Sun's Open Look and Motif on the VAX. All PC versions can access dBASE and Lotus 1-2-3 files in their native formats, but only the OS/2 and Windows versions can access ORACLE and other database servers through the EXSYS SQL Interface Package. This interface is actually a licensed version of Pioneer Software's Database Library (discussed in Chapter 5). The Unix versions can use any of the common Unix SQL databases, including ORACLE, Informix, Ingres, and Sybase SQL Server.

KBMS

Trinzic Corp.'s KBMS uses an advanced 4GL to build a graphics-based expert system. It features an easy-to-use application generator that insulates the application designer from writing programming code. Its main feature is a high-level natural-language interface that lets the user create queries in plain English. The interface makes its best attempt to translate an English query into the appropriate database language or SQL statements. If it can't quite understand what the user is asking, it will provide some suggestions for correcting the query, based on the columns in the database.

KBMS supports MS-DOS, Windows 3.*x*, and OS/2 on PCs. Versions are also available for various flavors of Unix, Digital's VAX/VMS, and IBM's mainframe-based VM and MVS. GUI versions are available for DECwindows, Open Look, and Motif.

KnowledgePro Windows

Knowledge Garden's KnowledgePro Windows, also known as KPWin, is a Windows 3.1–based object-oriented application development environment that also resembles an analysis tool as much as it does an expert system. KPWin uses a list processing language similar to LISP to manage complex information. (A *list processing* language uses a list of actions for the application to take, instead of the series of commands used in the typical 3GL and 4GL. List processing languages are commonly used for AI application development.) It also has many hypertext capabilities. It takes full advantage of Windows 3.1, including multimedia support and DDE. KPWin is designed primarily as a standalone application development tool used for adding expert-system capabilities to other Windows applications.

KPWin runs only on Windows 3.1; a version for Windows NT is under development. A licensed copy of Pioneer's Q&E Database Editor is included in the extra-cost KPWin SQL Kit to provide access to database files and servers.

NEXPERT Object

Neuron Data's NEXPERT Object is an object-oriented set of programming libraries and utilities for creating expert systems that run under Unix. It has its own graphical interface that makes it easy to edit rules, objects, and control structures. It also includes 3GL libraries that can embed expert-system functions into custom applications; support is provided for C, FORTRAN, Pascal, COBOL, and Ada. The Unified Database Bridge links NEXPERT Object applications to ORACLE databases, and it automatically handles any needed data mappings and SQL translations.

NEXPERT Object is available for a number of Unix variants, including Apollo UNIX, HP/UX, Digital's ULTRIX, IBM's RS/6000 AIX, and SUN Unix.

CASE/Design Tools

CASE (Computer Assisted System Engineering) is a class of applications that help system engineers and programmers design end-user applications. CASE tools range from those that generate pseudocode that the programmer can use as the basis for writing the application in a 3GL, to those that actually generate the final application in the appropriate 3GL or 4GL. There are a number of CASE applications available, but only two that are designed for C/S use with ORACLE.

Cadre DB Designer

Cadre Technologies makes a number of CASE tools that go by the Teamwork product series name, such as Teamwork/SA for system analysis and Teamwork/IM for information modeling. The Cadre DB Designer is a GUI database design tool that's not strictly a CASE tool; however, one of its primary features is that it works closely with Cadre's Teamwork CASE tools, so it fits into this category.

DB Designer can be used for both designing new relational databases or for *reengineering* (another term for downsizing) existing nonrelational databases to an RDBMS. Cadre's Data Driver Reengineering feature assists in designing a relational database by sampling existing databases and suggesting a structure for the new database. It can also deduce existing business rules from the current database to help in migrating the data to the new RDBMS. The Relational Expert feature helps you tune the new database for performance by reducing the database to a number of possible third normalization level designs. It also generates the appropriate SQL commands to create the database.

DB Designer also includes the Design by Example feature, which can be used as a prototyping tool prior to actually creating the database. It works in

conjunction with the other two features to help you find the best database design for performance and functionality. DB Designer can import CASE designs from the Teamwork products and can generate the appropriate SQL
DLLs for the target platform and DBMS.

DB Designer is available for OS/2 1.2 or higher, and also runs on Unix systems supporting the Open Look and Motif GUIs. It supports ORACLE,
IBM's DB2, Informix, Ingres, Digital's Rdb/VMS, and Sybase SQL Server,
and can also generate ANSI SQL Level 2 code for use with other RDBMSs.
However, it only supports ORACLE in a C/S environment at this time.

ERwin/ERX

Logic Works's ERwin/ERX is a superset of its ERwin/SQL front-end products that provide a GUI-based tool for designing C/S front ends for various
database servers; these include ORACLE, IBM's DB2, Gupta's SQLBase
Server, Informix 5.0, Ingres, Microsoft SQL Server, Sybase SQL Server, Net-
Ware SQL, and Digital's Rdb/VMS. ERwin/ERX features both forward and
reverse engineering capabilities; forward engineering lets you design the database and then create it based on the design. Reverse engineering lets you import the design and integrity rules from an existing database for further
development with ERwin/ERX. It calls the diagrams created during the reverse engineering process entity-relationship (ER) diagrams. It uses the drag-
and-drop features of the GUI as much as possible when creating tables, integrity and business rules, and indexes. ERwin/ERX can also create high-quality
reports on the database design and structure. ERwin/ERX can be used as a
limited CASE tool, or its ER diagrams and other program reports can be exported for use in a full-fledged CASE tool. It can also import information
from a CASE program.

ERwin/SQL is a scaled-down version of ERwin/ERX. The main difference between the two is that ERwin/SQL doesn't include the import/export
and reverse engineering capabilities.

ERwin/ERX is available for Windows 3.x, Apple's Macintosh, and Unix
implementations of Motif. An Intel 80386–based PC is the recommended minimum level. ERwin/SQL is available only for Windows 3.x.

Communications

The products in this section are not front ends; they're communications utilities that help you access an ORACLE database using C/S tools. In general,
they provide the networking protocols or data-access protocols needed to
communicate with a database residing on a host system that you otherwise
would have to access via a terminal.

Comten TCP/IP

NCR's Comten System 3000 Communications Processors are a popular type of network gateway processor used for many IBM mainframes. The System 3000 is based on a proprietary NCR chip set. It currently supports connections to Token Ring, Ethernet, and ISDN networks; connections to FDDI and ATM networks are under development. The system can also be expanded through external Multiple Connection Adapter Modules (MCAMs), which contain eight internal bus slots for the addition of NCR's Intel CPU-based communication expansion cards. The MCAM boxes use a SCSI attachment to the System 3000 and each other, and up to eight MCAMs can be daisy-chained together. This provides gateway capabilities for up to 100 LANs and 16 mainframes. The MCAM can also be used as a stand-alone TCP/IP network bridge. The Comten TCP/IP protocol suite runs on the System 3000 or MCAM, and provides TCP/IP access to databases running on an MVS or VM system. It automatically handles the appropriate gateway conversions between TCP/IP and the SNA protocols used by the mainframe.

A number of TCP/IP communications features are supported, including FTP (file transfer protocol), Sun's NFS (Network File System), and ORACLE's SQL*NET for TCP/IP. This lets you create C/S applications that can directly access an ORACLE database running on the mainframe. It also facilitates creating distributed databases with ORACLE servers running on TCP/IP-capable hosts.

DAL Server for UNIX

The Data Access Language (DAL) was designed by Apple Computer Corp. to work with the Data Access Manager (DAM) to give Macintoshes C/S capabilities. Pacer Software created DAL Server for UNIX to give DAL-compatible systems access to databases residing on Sun SPARC, HP-UX, IBM RS/6000, and Digital's ULTRIX systems. It works over both asynchronous (modem dial-in) and TCP/IP protocols. Macintoshes use the DAM to talk to the DAL client; PCs based on Intel chips can use the appropriate ODBC driver. The DAM uses its own version of SQL, and the DAL Server translates it into the native SQL used by the database server. Unix versions of ORACLE, Ingres, Informix, and Sybase SQL Server are supported.

DAL Server for UNIX runs on Sun SPARC systems, IBM RS/6000 AIX systems, HP 9000 systems running HP/UX, and Digital systems running ULTRIX.

Interlink Application Gateway-TCPaccess

Interlink Computer Sciences created Interlink Application Gateway-TCPaccess to provide TCP/IP links between a Digital VAX and an IBM mainframe running MVS. Application Gateway runs on the VAX under the VMS operating system. It lets systems running the TCP/IP version of SQL*NET go through the VAX to communicate with an ORACLE database on the mainframe. It also lets you create distributed database systems between the VMS version of ORACLE and the MVS version.

KNET NFS

Fibronics International's KNET NFS is a combined hardware and software product that provides TCP/IP access to an IBM mainframe running MVS or VM. KNET's hardware plugs into the mainframe and connects to a TCP/IP network running on either Ethernet or FDDI cables. It supports both SQL* NET connections to an ORACLE database running on the mainframe, and SQL*Connect connections to other databases on the mainframe.

Document and Image/Graphics Management

Document and image management applications help offices and corporations handle the volumes of text they produce each and every day. The original users of these applications were law offices, which immediately saw the benefits of quickly finding information about prior cases.

Document management systems usually work with one or more of the popular word processing applications available. The management system controls access to the documents, and it automatically creates a document information and history profile that lets the creator of the document give more complete details on what the document contains, who wrote it, and specify a set of keywords for quick searches on a particular topic. They also include a form of version control that tracks both the original document and any changed versions stored in the system, including information on who made the change. In recent years, document management systems have expanded their capabilities to include creating indexes of the text in the documents themselves, which lets users search for a particular word or phrase in all the documents stored in the system.

Image/graphics management systems are an enhancement to or variation on document management systems. They provide the same profiling and searching capabilities for documents stored in one of the many popular graphics formats. The images usually come from documents scanned with an Optical Character Recognition (OCR) scanner, or from faxes directly received by the computer through a fax board or fax modem.

The majority of document and image/graphics management systems use their own proprietary database structures for storing the profiles and indexes. However, a few vendors and VARs have created specialized management systems that use an ORACLE database or server as the database engine for storing the profiles or indexes.

AdaptFile Document Image Processing System

Adaptive Information Systems is a VAR that created AdaptFile Document Image Processing System as a PC LAN–based management system. It uses Hitachi imaging products, including the Hitachi OCR and various Hitachi read/write CD-ROM systems, for storing up to 10 million documents. Adapt-File uses an ORACLE version 6.0 database server as the database engine for indexing the documents and creating document profiles. ORACLE servers running on OS/2, Banyan's VINES, NetWare, or various Unix platforms are supported.

The AdaptFile software itself runs on PCs based on Intel chips. C/S communications are available over NetWare, VINES, LAN Manager, and LAN Server LANs. Adaptive Information Systems provides the ORACLE software, front end, and any Hitachi hardware systems required for a complete document and image managing system.

EasyFile 3000 and ExpressFile 7000

DocuPoint is another VAR that specializes in document retrieval and management systems. EasyFile 3000 is a standalone, Windows-based document management system that's particularly designed to store document images created with an OCR scanner. ExpressFile 7000 is a C/S document management and retrieval system that uses ORACLE as the database engine. Docu-Point provides its own read/write CD-ROM system for document and image storage for either system.

The ExpressFile 7000 front-end software supports Windows 3.*x*. The back-end system runs with the SCO UNIX version of ORACLE on any PC based on an Intel 386 or better CPU.

Feith Document Database

Feith Systems and Software is a VAR that created its own document and image management system based on a number of database servers. The Feith Document Database can work with an ORACLE Informix, Sybase SQL Server, or Gupta SQLBase database server to provide additional document management and indexing capabilities. Feith has also designed its own interface to a number of read/write CD-ROM systems.

Feith Document Database's front end runs under Windows 3.*x* over a NetWare LAN. It supports any Unix-based ORACLE database server that can be accessed through a NetWare LAN. Feith is currently developing a

Windows NT version of the package and will also support the NT version of ORACLE.

Metamorph

Thunderstone Software's Metamorph is a proprietary text search-and-retrieval system that lets users do fuzzy searches (searches based on part of a word or on similar-sounding words), numeric searches, and expressions. It also supports various wildcards. Metamorph can automatically import data from a live data feed, such as a stock-market update service. It interfaces with ORACLE databases through ORACLE's LONG datatype and can search for any text contained in a database. Searches can be done real-time or though indexes created at predetermined times.

Metamorph runs on DOS, Macintosh, Windows 3.1, VAX/VMS, PRIM-EOS (Prime Computers), and Data General/MV systems. A number of Unix implementations are also supported. Metamorph can access any version of ORACLE supported by the appropriate SQL*NET drivers.

Metamorph can run as a standalone system, or can be used with Thunderstone's 3DB text index database. 3DB makes text searches faster, and provides support for up to four billion text files containing up to four billion characters each. An API package that lets application developers integrate the Metamorph text retrieval engine into their own applications is also available. The API supports the C language.

Metabook

Metabook is a special version of Metamorph designed for book or manual text files. It automatically creates a table of contents for the document being searched and is designed for use with on-line program documentation files or help files. Figure 8.1 shows Metabook's simple interface and the results of a multiword query.

PRC Technical Document Management System

Planning Research Corp. is a well known VAR that provides a variety of customized applications for various industries, particularly the U.S. Government and the real-estate industry. PRC Technical Document Management System is designed primarily for engineering and manufacturing companies that need to keep track of design documents and engineering drawings and blueprints. It supports OCR images and text files, and it can access files stored on standalone or networked disks or on a number of read/write CD-ROM systems. It uses ORACLE as the indexing and retrieval database.

Figure 8.1

Metabook is a simplified version of Metamorph, designed for use with on-line manuals or documentation.

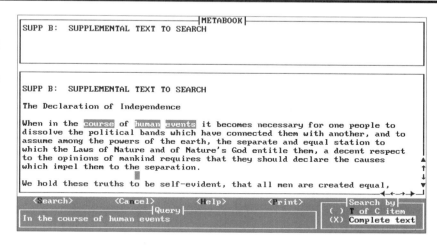

PRC Technical Document Management System runs on MS-DOS and OS/2 PCs over NetWare or VINES LANs. It also supports a number of Unix systems, including Apollo's Unix, Sun's Unix, Digital's ULTRIX, IBM's AIX, and HP/UX. Versions are also available for Digital's VAX/VMS and Data General computers.

PRC's Image Management System

PRC also sells a general-purpose Image Management System designed for small offices or large corporations. This system is actually more of an image management engine, with its own API that can be used to create custom front-end applications. It also uses ORACLE as the indexing and retrieval database engine.

Custom front ends can be created on any platform that can talk to the Image Management System server. Versions of the server are available for NetWare, OS/2, VINES, HP/UX, ULTRIX, VAX/VMS, AIX, and Sun's Unix.

Topic

Verity's Topic is designed from the ground up for distributed-processing text management and retrieval. Topic features an advanced text search capability that Verity calls concept retrieval. *Concept retrieval* lets users create and store queries that can be used to search and retrieve only documents related to a particular topic. Its front end integrates into a number of popular word processing and desktop publishing systems running on Intel chip–based PCs,

Macintoshes, and various Unix systems. A menu-driven front end is also available for integrating other applications into Topic. It features an English-like query language for searching profiles and stored documents. Topic provides its own indexing and profiling database; however, it can access ORACLE and other database servers through the Topic SQL-Bridge and SQL-Gateway modules that are available for an additional cost.

The Topic Real-Time add-on module integrates real-time data acquisition systems into a Topic system. The Topic SDK lets application developers integrate the Topic search engine into their applications. It also uses the C language.

Topic runs on MS-DOS, Windows 3.*x*, Macintosh, OS/2, VAX/VMS, and various Unix implementations. It works over NetWare, VINES, NFS, LAN Server, DECNet, and LAN Manager networks.

Vertical-Market Applications

THERE COMES A TIME IN ALMOST EVERY COMPANY'S LIFE WHEN IT NEEDS a highly specialized computer application to fill a particular need. It's then faced with three choices: Have the in-house programming staff develop the application from the ground up, hire a consultant to write it from the ground up, or purchase the application. A large corporation may not have a problem with the first choice, but a smaller business probably doesn't have an in-house staff. And if the needed application is very specific to a particular part of the business, the company may have difficulty finding a local consultant with enough expertise in that particular area to write the application in a reasonable amount of time.

In many cases, the best choice is to purchase a specialized application. Such applications are commonly known as vertical-market applications, because they're designed to fill a particular need in a particular industry. The ORACLE RDBMS has been available for over a decade now, and there's a wide variety of vertical-market applications available from third-party software vendors and VARs. These applications run the gamut from accounting packages to those designed for the health care, manufacturing, and retail industries.

Many vertical-market applications started out as systems designed to run on a host computer accessed through dedicated terminals; in recent years, though, the software developers have recognized the benefits of the C/S architecture and moved their applications to it. The products covered in this chapter can all run on a C/S system. Some of them can also run as standalone or host-based systems. And in some cases, the vertical-market application is actually a total solution that includes all the necessary hardware and software to run the system.

I've placed each product into the category it best seems to fit in, or the category the vendor thinks best describes the product's market. Please note that the presence or absence of a product or company name in this chapter in no way implies an endorsement or criticism of that product or company. You should use the information on vertical-market applications presented here as a starting point for your own search for and evaluation of specialized applications for your business.

Evaluating Vertical-Market Applications

The first thing to do, of course, is decide if you want to spend the time and money needed to have your in-house programmers create the application. If you decide against this (or if you don't have an in-house programming staff), the next step is to start looking for an appropriate vertical-market application.

There are three starting points for evaluating a specialized application based on ORACLE for your business. The first is if you already use ORACLE and want to add the application to an existing system. Since it's less complicated to continue using a system you're already familiar with, your best bet is to go with an application like the ones listed here.

The second starting point would be where you already have an application, but it no longer has the horsepower needed to keep up with your expanding needs. Perhaps you have a system based on a traditional PC-based DBMS, such as dBASE or Paradox, that's slowing down because of the number of users or volume of data. Or you might have a host-based system that doesn't support access from LAN users. With this latter case, you have a choice of vertical-market applications that includes many more products than just those based on ORACLE. On the other hand, you don't want to lose all the data you already have in the existing system, so the range of potential products is narrowed to those that provide either an easy way to integrate the existing system into the new one, or a way to migrate to the new system without seriously affecting day-to-day operations.

Finally, you may not have a computerized system at all, in which case your choices are virtually unlimited. ORACLE is only one of many client/server RDBMSs available today, and there are vertical-market applications available for all the different database servers. This is the most complex starting point of the three, so you should expect to spend a lot of time investigating and choosing the right system.

One advantage of buying a vertical-market application is that the vendors are usually very flexible, and are willing to customize their software for your particular needs. You should certainly expect to pay more for this service, but it's nice to know that a critical application can grow and evolve as your business needs expand or change.

The last point to bear in mind is to keep your expectations realistic. No application package or system is perfect. Finding the right one for your business is more often a case of finding the best fit than it is of finding one that solves all your problems. Remain open to the possibility that you many not find an application that does everything you need, and that some customization may be needed. And finally, keep open to the possibility that you may have to modify your own business procedures to get the best use from the application you select.

Perform a Needs Analysis

Regardless of where you're starting from, you should keep in mind some very basic but important points. The first and most important is to have as clear an idea as you can of what it is you want the application to do for you. The better you state your goals, the better chance the software vendors and VARs have of knowing if their products fit your needs. If your goals aren't clear, you may waste a lot of time by investigating applications that don't really do what you need done.

One common way to state your goals is to create and give to potential vendors a request for proposals (RFP). This document clearly states what type of system you need and what you expect the vendor to install, service, and support. RFPs are discussed in the section "The Evaluation Process," later in this chapter.

Finding potential applications is relatively easy. In addition to the information in this chapter, you should be able to get information on specialized applications from business associates, or from the many national associations that represent particular industries. Trade shows and conventions are another good source of information on applications for your particular industry.

Consult End Users

The second important thing to do is the one most often overlooked when searching for a specialized application. Get the ultimate users of the application involved in the selection process early on. Users include everyone who may have to rely on the application to do their jobs, from the personnel who enter the data to the managers who use it to monitor the business. Unfortunately, there are too many cases where the search for a vertical-market application starts when a manager goes to one of the computer support staff members and simply says, "Find us an application that does this." The person charged with the search probably isn't familiar with the internal operations of the department that will be using the application. Or perhaps the person may be in the department but only familiar with one aspect of what the application should do.

Forming a Search Committee

There are many clichés that disparage work done by a committee. However, selecting a vertical-market application is one case where a committee made up of representatives of all the potential users can significantly improve the process. A committee helps you figure out a clear goal for the application, as everyone who will ultimately rely on the application can state what their needs are up front. The committee can jointly agree on what the application should do, and create the RFP to give to the vendors.

A committee also spreads the burden of finding potential applications. With more people looking for them, the odds increase that you'll find an application that works for you.

Finally, the search committee should be involved in the selection process. The committee members should be the ones to sit down with the vendors and get all the details on the various products available. The committee should then evaluate the various proposals received, ask the vendors for more information if necessary, and prepare a recommendation for the organization's senior management on which product to purchase.

The Evaluation Process

Buying a vertical-market application is a more complex process than just buying a piece of software off the shelf at your local software store. In Chapter 8 I discussed some points to keep in mind about VARs; the same points apply here, since just about all of the applications in this chapter come from VARs.

Once you've done your search and found the applications you would like to investigate further, it's time to approach the vendors. The first step is to send them a copy of the RFP your committee has drawn up. At the minimum, the RFP should contain the following information:

- A brief overview of your company, including the primary business market it's in.

- An overview statement of what type of application you're looking for.

- The particular business problems you would like the application to solve.

- A listing of any hardware platforms and software applications that you're already using. If you don't have an existing system yet, list the hardware and software platforms you would prefer to use.

- A request for references—names of other customers using the vendor's product.

- The date by which you must receive the vendor's response.

- The hours and days of the week you expect to need support for the application.

- Any training you would like to have on the application, both for your in-house technical staff and for the end users of the application.

- A copy of or reference to any laws or purchasing regulations that apply if you're a government entity.

Send at least one copy to the vendors you've selected. When you've received all the replies, it's time to start evaluating the products. Some vendors may not have responded, or they may have sent you a letter explaining that they decline to participate in the process because their products don't fit your requirements; you can cross them off your list.

If you don't get any responses from any of the vendors, however, you should sit down and reevaluate your RFP. You may find that your requirements are so narrow or so strict that no one can meet them (remember what I said about keeping realistic expectations). It may help to contact a couple of the vendors and find out why they declined to respond; this should help you get a better idea of what to ask for.

Once you have your responses in hand, you should particularly watch for the following points:

- **Support:** *Does each vendor provide the support you need, especially during the hours you need it?* You may not need support 24 hours a day, seven days a week. However, you should watch out for support hours that significantly differ from your normal working hours.

  Another point to look for is each vendor's proposed response time. Support 24 hours a day does you no good if the vendor's support staff takes more than a day to get back to you after your initial call. If the system is mission-critical to your business, you will need a response time of a working day or less.

  You should also see whether the vendor just provides general support or if it assigns a particular support person to your account. The latter is the better option, as you're sure of getting support from a person who's already familiar with your business environment.

- **Customization:** *Does the vendor provide programming services to customize the application for your particular situation?* Most vertical-market application vendors will work with you to make sure the application does what you want it to do, and will comply with any reasonable requests for custom features. The tricky part is agreeing on what's reasonable. You'll also need to agree on what customization services are included in the original contract, and which ones are provided at additional cost.

- **Source code:** *What provisions are made for your access to the source code if need be?* Software companies do go out of business, and you don't want to be stuck with no way to maintain a mission-critical application. The vendor should at the minimum propose that the source code be stored in a neutral site such as a bank vault, to be released to you should the vendor go out of business. The proposal (and eventually the contract) should contain a clause that specifies that vendor will keep the stored copy of the source code up to date, with the same changes made to your copy of the application.

  You might also consider having the same protection for discontinued products. Vendors usually stop supporting discontinued products after a certain amount of time passes. Make sure the vendor's proposal makes provisions for releasing the source code to you should this happen.

- **Installation:** *Does the vendor just ship a bunch of boxes and disks to you, or does it send one or more support engineers or technicians to your site to set up the application and ensure that it's running?* The lack of in-house personnel capable of writing a specialized application is one of the main reasons behind buying it from a third party. The vendor should at least provide priority telephone tech support during the installation period. Better yet, the vendor should send its own personnel to your site to set the system up for you, or to work with your in-house staff to get it running.

- **Training:** *Does the vendor provide on-site user training, or do you have to ship your personnel to a central training site?* The former is the better choice from a cost standpoint, especially for organizations that anticipate having a large number of application users.

  Also, does the vendor provide training for your own support personnel? The cost of support training can easily be offset by the reduction in system downtime; the in-house staff can take care of the minor problems that would otherwise require a call to the vendor.

- **Updates:** *What provisions does the vendor make for providing updates or bug fixes for the application? And what about upgrades?* You shouldn't have to search frantically to find the periodic updates most vendors make to their products. At the least, you should be notified of when they're available and what they add to the product, even if there's an additional fee involved. Of course, updates that are strictly bug fixes should be sent to you immediately, and without any charge.

The next step is to meet with the vendor's representatives to get a better understanding of the product and its capabilities. The vendor should also provide you with a live demonstration of the system, either at your offices or in a demonstration center the vendor has set up. Your committee members should have the opportunity to try the application themselves, to get a feel for how it works and whether it does what they need.

You should also contact some or all of the vendor's other clients that were provided as references, to get their opinions on the application and the vendor's support. If they're willing to do so, these references might even let you send a representative to their site to take a look at the system in action. Someone who's already using the application for daily business activities can give you valuable information on the strengths and weaknesses of a particular package.

Accounting and Financial

This category of applications is pretty much self-explanatory. These applications are designed to automate a company's financial systems, such as payrolls, billing, and taxes. They can also be used for project cost management, keeping track of assets, and bad-debt collections. In some cases the applications presented here can be run either by themselves or as an integrated part of a more extensive system of applications sold by the same vendor.

ALCIE IV

ALCIE IV series, from CD Data Corp., is a financial package aimed at the distribution and manufacturing industries, though others may find it useful (distribution applications are covered in the next section of this chapter). ALCIE stands for Assets, Liabilities, Capital, Income, and Expense. The system is written entirely with ORACLE Tools and is based on ORACLE, version 6.0. It consists of a number of modules, such as Menu, Accounts Payable, Accounts Receivable, General Ledger, Payroll, Purchase Order, and Fixed Assets—a total of 14 modules in all. It can be run as is, or CD DATA will customize it to fit a particular client's needs.

Since it's written using Oracle Corp.'s toolkits, ALCIE IV is compatible with any platform supported by ORACLE, and it can be run on a dedicated host PC or in a C/S system.

Axtell Fixed Assets

Axtell Development Corp.'s Axtell Fixed Assets is designed for any organization that needs to keep track of assets for depreciation and tax purposes. Like ALCIE IV, it's also written entirely with ORACLE Tools. According to the vendor, the software's strongest features are its reporting functions, which cover the standard tax and book depreciation methods, as well as its ability to print the appropriate IRS tax forms automatically. User-defined depreciation methods are also supported, and the company will customize the program as needed.

Axtell Fixed Assets can run on any platform ORACLE supports, in host mode or as a C/S system. If you don't already have ORACLE, the company provides complete systems that run on HP-UX, NetWare, or SCO MPX Unix.

Banner Finance System

Systems & Computer Technology Corp. aims its Banner Finance System at the government and education markets. Banner provides common financial functions, such as a general ledger, purchasing and receiving, fixed assets, and cost accounting. The program can provide these functions on an organization-wide level, or on a department level with a central point of integration for all the subsystems. Banner Human Resources System is an add-on module that integrates the personnel department records into the financial system. Banner also has three other modules designed specifically for the education market:

- The Banner Financial Aid System

- The Banner Student System

- The Banner Alumni/Development System

These modules can be run on their own but work best when integrated with the main package.

Banner Finance System is primarily designed to be run with ORACLE on a multiuser Unix host. However, Systems & Computer Technology can also set up a C/S system with a network running TCP/IP to a Unix-based database server.

MT/PSMS

Management Technologies's MT/PSMS is actually a staff and project management system that includes complete cost accounting. It's primarily aimed at the professional services industry. It can track weekly tasks, employee time sheets and assignments, and the documents associated with a project. MT/PSMS can also create invoices for a project, and create a complete set of management reports for tracking project costs and profitability.

MT/PSMS started out as a VAX-based system, and was moved to the C/S architecture within the last two years. It is currently designed and programmed in Powersoft's Powerbuilder, so it only runs on Windows 3.x systems. It supports any ORACLE server through the SQL*NET communications protocol.

Recovery 1

Recovery 1, from Fiest Data Recovery, is a loan tracking and recovery application aimed at banks, credit agencies, or any organization that needs to track and recover bad debts. Its various components cover collection activities, audits, and bankruptcy tracking. The application is menu driven, and features standard or user-defined data tables, forms, and reports.

Recovery 1 runs on OS/2, VAX/VMS, and IBM AIX systems. It can run in multiuser host mode or as a C/S system on OS/2 clients.

SQL*TIME Financials

Design Data Systems Corp. specializes in creating applications for companies in the distribution and sales markets. Each SQL*TIME application covers a distinct aspect of this field and is a complete standalone application, so the rest will be covered in the appropriate category. However, all SQL*TIME applications can share the same database to create a customized integrated system.

SQL*TIME Financials provides both standard and user-defined accounting capabilities, as well as project-cost management and accounting functions. It includes a number of forecasting capabilities, audit trails, cash projections, and collection management. It can even print checks.

All of the SQL*TIME applications are programmed with ORACLE Tools, so they support any ORACLE platform in multiuser host mode or in the C/S architecture. The company is currently moving the applications to version 7.0 of ORACLE and the new releases of ORACLE Tools.

Distribution Systems

Distribution is a broad category that covers anything having to do with storing and shipping manufactured items. The programs in this category can be used to run a warehouse, or to track the sales and distribution of items that are manufactured as needed. In some cases, these applications can be integrated with others from the same vendor that keep financial records, assist sales departments in making client contacts, or track the actual manufacturing process.

CIID

CIID (Computer Interactive Integrated Distribution), by Avalon Software, is a complete distribution system aimed primarily at organizations with multiple distribution sites or subsidiary companies. CIID can run on a single database server or in a distributed environment.

CIID's primary functions include inventory control, order processing and management, and accounts receivable. The inventory module supports the just-in-time (JIT) method of manufacturing, where products aren't assembled until needed for shipment. JIT manufacturing helps keep inventory costs down and is becoming a popular method for creating durable goods. The complete source code is included in the price of the product.

CIID is primarily designed for multiuser, single- or multihost systems. However, it supports Macintoshes as the front end for a C/S system, or a mixed terminal and client system.

JIT Distribution System

Just in Time Enterprise Systems specializes in computer systems for organizations that use the JIT method of manufacturing. Its JIT Distribution System can be used by itself or as part of a complete manufacturing system composed of the other JIT applications discussed in the section on manufacturing, later in this chapter.

The bulk of JIT Distribution System is written in Oracle's SQL*Forms, so the system can be used on any host or C/S platform supported by ORACLE. It supports both single and multiple site organizations through distributed databases. It provides inventory control, support for multiple sources of supplies, and uses historical sales trends for statistical forecasting of product demand. It can also track multiple shipping points for a single order, and warranties. JIT Distribution System can read and use bar code data for inventory management.

The software is primarily a C/S application that runs on any client supported by Oracle's SQL*Forms, including MS-DOS, OS/2, the Macintosh, and various flavors of Unix. The server side can be any ORACLE platform.

SQL*TIME Distribution

SQL*TIME Distribution is the second major module in Design Data Systems Corp.'s SQL*TIME applications. This model manages inventory functions, including multiple warehouses, order tracking, product pricing, and delivery time tracking. It can be used as a standalone system, or integrated with SQL* TIME Financials to provide automatic accounting information from the warehouses to the central organization.

Other SQL*TIME modules aimed at distribution management can be purchased separately, or can work together with SQL*TIME Distribution to provide additional functions. These modules are SQL*TIME Order Entry, SQL*TIME Purchase Order, and SQL*TIME Inventory. The SQL*TIME system is aimed at the telemarketing, manufacturing, and distribution industries.

All SQL*TIME applications are programmed using ORACLE Tools, so they support any client system and database server supported by ORACLE.

Education

Education is another broad category when it comes to computer automation. The applications in this section range from those that provide actual classroom instruction to those that track student classes and grades to those that map school districts.

Conference Services and Housing Information System

Applied Collegiate Systems sells two applications aimed at colleges and universities. Conference Services is designed for scheduling and managing conferences and seminars. It tracks open and in-use conference rooms and equipment, registrations and attendance, and account billing and receivables. It also features merge capabilities with many popular word processing packages, making it easy to send out information letters and schedules to conference attendees. It can work with Housing Information System to track and manage temporary housing for those attending the conference.

Housing Information System manages all aspects of on- and off-campus housing run by a college or university. It keeps track of facilities and residents, and building maintenance and inventories. It can automatically assign rooms based on user-defined criteria. It also includes billing and account-receivable functions. The data can be exported into a number of standard formats to be imported into other student or financial systems.

The two systems are primarily designed to run on a multiuser VAX/VMS system, though they can also be run on an Intel chip–based PC running Interactive 386 Unix. The client systems can run MS-DOS or OS/2, using the TCP/IP version of SQL*NET to talk to the server.

MapNET Boundary Planning and Redistricting

Ecotran Systems specializes in mapping applications for government use. MapNET Boundary Planning and Redistricting tracks and maps school districts. It can be used to realign districts to more closely follow the student population, or as a decision support system to determine which schools need greater or lesser resources. It stores a number of different data items about each student, including school grades, gender, and race, and can be used to align school districts with demographic attendance plans.

It also has an integrated module that lets school district administrators do "what if" projections based on present and future birth rates, population changes, and housing starts. This module can be used for planning long-range school and resource needs.

A related application is MapNET Bus Routing, which provides for the routing, scheduling, and maintenance of school buses. It can automatically create bus stops based on student population distribution while taking safety and traffic concerns into account.

The primary and most common front end for MapNET is based on OS/2, with the rest on MS-DOS. The server is based on an Intel 80486 system running the OS/2 or NLM version of ORACLE. MapNET can also support an HP 9000 running HP-UX as the server.

RIMS

Jostens Learning Corp.'s RIMS (Renaissance Instructional Management System) is an instructional system based on ORACLE, with Apple Macintosh front ends. It includes the Jostens Basic Learning System, which is composed of over 1,800 reading and math lessons for the kindergarten through 8th grade levels. RIMS can track each student's progress through the lessons. The system can also be customized to provide a particular lesson sequence, and it can be expanded to include other learning systems on other subjects.

RIMS currently runs on a Macintosh or Unix database server with Macintosh client systems. The company is working on porting the client system to Windows 3.x, and the server to Windows NT and possibly other ORACLE servers.

STAR_BASE

STAR_BASE, from Century Consultants, is a student record system for secondary schools. It consists of 15 separate modules, including student scheduling, attendance reporting, grade reporting, class scheduling and rosters, and tracking standardized tests. It can create a number of optional reports for local administration use, and mandatory reports required by the various state education departments. Century Consultants customizes the program for the particular state the client school system is in.

The STAR_BASE server runs on a number of Unix systems, including IBM's AIX and NCR Unix. The front end primarily runs on a Macintosh, though an MS-DOS version is available.

Health Care

Applications for the health care field are primarily concerned with patient information tracking or clinical drug trials. They're used to store patient medical data or assign hospital rooms; they may also include financial functions to track patient billing. A subset of these applications support the pharmaceutical industry in tracking patient reactions to drugs during clinical trials.

ARIS

ARIS (Adverse Reaction Information System) is one of five applications sold by Clinical Information Services for the pharmaceutical industry. It tracks adverse patient reactions to drugs and also creates the appropriate reports for the FDA and other national and international drug regulatory agencies. The application can also be used to create ad hoc reports, and it can interface with SAS for statistical studies. The other four applications made by Clinical Information Services are:

- CLIN.GCP—Clinical Trials Management System is a related application that interfaces with ARIS and plans, tracks, and controls the clinical trial process for a new drug. It's primarily a system for project management and financial planning, since it tracks the clinics and patients involved in the drug studies. It can create the appropriate reports needed for drug approvals by regulatory agencies, and the data can be used by ARIS for continued tracking of the product after release.

- CLIN.DB—Clinical Trials Data Management System is a scaled-down version of CLIN.GCP that just tracks and reports on clinical trials. It's a standalone that doesn't interface with any of the other applications.

- PCRS—Product Complaint Report System is used to register and track complaints about pharmaceutical products, as required by the FDA. The complaints can be categorized as medical, technical, or other. PCRS interfaces with ARIS to assist in tracking adverse reactions to drugs.

- PILLS—Package Insert Labeling & Logistics System interfaces with ARIS and PCRS to create the appropriate package inserts for a drug's packaging. PILLS is actually a specialized document management system that can store package inserts as images, OCR documents, and word-processing text. It supports full-text searches, global revisions of inserts, and incorporates desktop publishing capabilities for printing the inserts. It also supports multiple languages, so it can be used on a worldwide basis.

With the exception of PCRS, all of Clinical Information Services products run on a VAX/VMS or Unix server in host or C/S mode. PCRS only runs on VMS at this time. DOS or OS/2 client workstations can be used in a C/S system.

CLINTROL

Computer Financial Corp.'s CLINTROL is a clinical trials management package for pharmaceutical companies. It tracks drugs that are currently in the approval process, and creates the appropriate reports for the FDA and other drug regulatory agencies. CLINTROL's chief feature is that it can gather the data directly from a PC in a physician's or clinic's office, speeding the data collection process and reducing the need to reenter the information. The application automatically verifies the format and accuracy of the remote data before incorporating it into the master database.

CLINTROL is primarily a host-based system that can run on a VAX/VMS, IBM RS 6000/AIX, or OS/2 system. It provides limited C/S capabilities through its remote data collection capabilities, so it merits mention here.

DSI Financial/Accounting System

DeLair Systems's DSI Financial/Accounting System is a specialized accounting system designed for use by hospitals, clinics, and other health care facilities, so I've included it here instead of with the other accounting packages. Its specialized functions include accounts receivable and payable, check writing, and facilities management. It also includes patient billing and payroll functions. All the sub-modules interface directly with a central general ledger. It supports standard and user-defined reports, and can export data to a Lotus 1-2-3 spreadsheet for further analysis, charting, and "what if" projections.

DSI also sells the DSI Patient Accounting/Receivables Management System, which has specific functions for managing patient accounts. It can be used in conjunction with the Financial/Accounting System to provide a complete financial management system for a health care facility.

These packages are written using the standard ORACLE Tools, so they support all the clients and servers supported by the ORACLE DBMS. They can run in host or C/S mode.

PCMS

PCMS (Patient Care Management System), by Q.S., is designed for use by health care clinics, community health care departments, and hospital outpatient clinics. Its numerous modules include support for patient billing, scheduling, laboratory support, pharmacy tracking, and patient tracking. It also includes support for general ledger functions, such as accounts payable and payrolls. It creates the appropriate reports needed for state and federal health care tracking agencies. The modules are integrated, and the user can use any or all of them as needed.

PCMS runs on an IBM AS/400 using IBM's AIX and the AIX version of ORACLE. The client systems are PCs based on MS-DOS.

VITALNET

Critikon is a subsidiary of Johnson & Johnson Company, a well-known name in the health care field. Its VITALNET is a network-based patient management system designed for use at the patient's bedside. It supports direct entry of patient information by the attending nurse. The data can be used for determining staff requirements and patient scheduling. It can also be used by the attending physicians for making decisions concerning appropriate medical strategies. Critikon sells VITALNET as a complete hardware and software system; the hardware can be interfaced to other medical monitors to provide real-time data collection of a patient's vital signs.

VITALNET runs on a NetWare LAN, with either the NLM or OS/2 versions of ORACLE. The client systems run on MS-DOS.

Human Resources

Human resources is currently the name for what has always been known as personnel departments. The sheer volume of information a human resources department has to maintain these days to satisfy the many state and federal labor law requirements makes them a prime candidate for computerization. Two of the many human resources packages or human resource management systems (HRMS) available today are based on ORACLE.

Empire/SQL

Empire/SQL, from Humanic Design Corp., stores over 1,500 different data items per employee record. It offers support for complete records on personnel information, analysis and reporting on salaries and wages, attendance tracking, application and résumé tracking, and performance-evaluation tracking. It can administrate 401K pension plans, COBRA and other employee benefit plans, and employee training and tuition assistance plans. It tracks

 **Manufacturing**

equal employment opportunity (EEO) and affirmative action program (AAP) information for complying with state and federal labor and EEO/AAP regulations. An optional payroll module is also available.

Humanic Design Corp. is a consulting firm that specializes in supporting human resources departments. Company representatives state that the best feature of their software is the long-term experience the company brings to the human resources field.

Empire/SQL is written entirely in ORACLE Tools, so it's available for all the platforms supported by the ORACLE RDBMS. It can be run as a standalone system, but the company says that the most common modes are host-based or client/server. The most common front ends are based on MS-DOS, and an OS/2-based client system is also available. The company is currently working on moving Empire/SQL to ORACLE, version 7.0.

PS/HRMS

PS/HRMS, from PeopleSoft, is a combination human resource, payroll, and benefits management application, currently supporting organizations in the United States and Canada. A European version is under development. It supports employee record keeping, resource planning, tax processing, direct deposits, tracking benefits and COBRA, and labor relations. It also keeps and reports on the information needed for the various state and federal labor regulations, such as EEO and AAP.

PS/HRMS runs only in C/S mode, using any ORACLE database server. The client software is custom-written by PeopleSoft and runs only on Windows 3.x.

Manufacturing

The specialized applications for the manufacturing industry cover many different facets, from assembly-line control to quality control to financial records and analysis. Manufacturing also doesn't just cover durable goods such as cars, computers, or refrigerators; there's a class of applications designed for the software market that tracks both the development process and bug reports.

Some of the applications in this section interface with those I've already covered under the accounting or distribution headings. Others provide the same features as those previously covered, but are designed primarily for this market, so they're included here instead of under the earlier headings.

Aurum-QualityTrak

Aurum Software's Aurum-QualityTrak is designed to monitor problems with software applications. It keeps track of bug reports, including the release number of the product affected. It also tracks source-code modules and can correlate the bug reports to the source-code module involved. It can store technical bulletins and act as a central lookup source for technical and client support personnel.

Aurum-SupportTrak is a related support tracking program designed to work either on its own or in conjunction with Aurum-QualityTrak. It tracks customer support calls to an inside technical-support department. It can also be used to track field-service calls. It can automatically log calls, issue dispatch orders for field engineers, and generate return material authorization (RMA) numbers. Aurum-SupportTrak can also track and maintain service contracts, and automatically issue renewal notices.

Aurum-QualityTrak and Aurum-SupportTrak run on the Unix versions of ORACLE, in multiuser host or C/S mode. The C/S front-end application requires Windows 3.x or a Unix GUI such as Motif or Open Look.

CIIM

CIIM (Computer Interactive Integrated Manufacturing) is Avalon Software's manufacturing application designed to work as a standalone, or in an integrated system with Avalon's CIID (covered in the section on distribution applications). CIIM consists of 14 modules that provide purchase-order functions, inventory management (including JIT methods), shop-floor control and scheduling, and capacity-requirement planning.

It also includes a number of financial functions, including fixed-assets management and general ledger. Complete accounting and financial functions are provided by Avalon's Computer Interactive Financial Accounting System (CIFAS). CIFAS can be used alone, or in a complete system with CIID and CIIM. Source code is provided for all of Avalon's applications.

Like CIID, CIIM and CIFAS are primarily designed for multiuser, single- or multihost systems. However, they all support Macintoshes as the front end for a C/S system, or mixed terminal and client systems.

EMIS

Electronic Manufacturing Information System (EMIS) is a set of 15 integrated modules created by ESI Technologies. Each module can be purchased and run on its own or as part of a complete computerized manufacturing system. The various EMIS modules are

- Accounts Payable System
- Accounts Receivable System
- Bill of Material
- Forecast Management System

- General Ledger System
- Integrated Accounting
- Manufacturing Solution
- Master Production Schedule
- Material Requirements Planning
- Order Processing Management System
- Product Configurator System
- Production Management System
- Quoting and Estimating Management System
- Sales Order Management System
- Serial Lot Bin Control System

EMIS is written 100 percent in ORACLE SQL and PL/SQL, so any ORACLE-compatible front end can be used. ESI-Technologies states that most of its clients use EMIS on a host-based system, but the company has its own Windows 3.x front end that runs over NetWare to the EMIS system on a Hewlett-Packard minicomputer running HP-UX.

Impression

Eyring Corp.'s Impression is a sophisticated application designed for use on the manufacturing floor. It manages work orders, routing, and data collection. Its most impressive feature is the ability to create, store, and display full-color assembly instructions, including pictures of the parts and text describing the assembly process. The main purpose behind the application is to improve quality control while decreasing the amount of time it takes to assemble a product.

Impression is strictly a C/S application, with DOS or Unix workstations acting as the front end, and an ORACLE server running on OS/2, NetWare, SCO MPX Unix, or HP-UX on the back end.

ICIM

ICIM (Interactive Computer Integrated Manufacturing), from Metasystems, is a manufacturing control system that consists of two major subsystems:

- The Interactive Customer Order Servicing (ICOS) subsystem provides the order processing, accounting, and sales tracking functions. The accounting functions include accounts receivable, accounts payable, and general ledger.

■ The Interactive Manufacturing Planning and Control (IMPACS) subsystem covers the actual manufacturing process, from start to finish.

ICIM can be used to support a single company location or used to form a complete distributed control system for organizations with multiple subsidiary companies, sites, or both.

ICIM is written entirely in Oracle Corp.'s SQL*Forms, so it can run on any client or server platform that ORACLE supports. It can also run in a multiuser host-based system.

Just-in-Time Manufacturing System

Just in Time Resources International's Just-in-Time Manufacturing System provides support for the JIT method of product assembly, ensuring that the materials are delivered only as they're needed. It provides work-order reporting, materials routing, and vendor tracking functions.

Other JIT modules that work with Just-in-Time Manufacturing System or as standalone applications include:

■ The Discrete Manufacturing System

■ The Finance System

■ The Process Manufacturing System

■ The Repetitive Processing Manufacturing System

All of the JIT modules are C/S applications that run on any client supported by Oracle's SQL*Forms, including MS-DOS, OS/2, Macintosh, and various flavors of Unix. The server side can be any ORACLE platform. The company also sells JIT Graphical User Interface, which lets users have multiple screens into the JIT databases open simultaneously. JIT Graphical User Interface runs under Windows 3.x.

Manufacturing Inventory Management System

Wellington Systems's Manufacturing Inventory Management System is an application that provides costing, bill of materials, work-order planning and scheduling, and purchase-order functions. The system can be customized for a particular client's needs. It's designed to be as user-friendly as possible, and makes extensive use of the Macintosh interface, including pull-down menus and pick lists.

The front-end software runs on a Macintosh; the back end can be any platform supported by ORACLE. Wellington representatives report that the most common back ends run on Hewlett-Packard, Digital VAX, and Macintosh systems.

Public Sector (Government)

It's an unfortunate fact of life that in a time of tight budgets, computerization is the first item to be put on the back burner in most government or public-sector agencies. However, there are a number of vendors that specialize in public-sector applications that increase the efficiency of providing government services while reducing the costs of those services.

CASS

CASS, from RJN Computer Services, is a set of three public-sector applications aimed at public-works departments. These applications are listed below:

- CASS WORKS SEWER is designed to assist in the maintenance and modeling of city sewers, and provides for scheduling routine preventive maintenance. It also collects the results of physical inspections of the sewer system, and it can download the appropriate data collected on-site with laptop or hand-held computers. It can also interface with a TV-based inspection system, to correlate written reports with the videotaped images.

- CASS WORKS STORMWATER is a similar system designed to manage storm-drain systems. It can schedule preventive maintenance or create maintenance work orders based on citizen complaints.

- CASS WORKS WATER provides maintenance scheduling and modeling for water systems. It can also monitor and model the capacity of the system, based on water pressure and usage.

All three systems also provide cost-accounting functions to assist the public works agency in preparing budgets for maintaining or expanding the water system.

The front end for the CASS systems runs on MS-DOS computers, using a proprietary interface developed by RJN. Any ORACLE server is supported on the back end, though the most common back ends are based on VAX/VMS and Unix systems.

Public-Works Applications

Hansen Software has written five public-works applications:

- Electric Distribution Management System (EDMS) provides for the control and maintenance of electric distribution lines. It can maintain inventories of electric poles, transformers, meters, switches, relays, street lights, and batteries. It automatically generates work orders based on user-defined preventive maintenance schedules or citizen complaints.

- Gas Distribution Management System (GDMS) provides similar functions for maintaining underground gas lines. It tracks storage sites and pumps by size; installation date; and pipe type, diameter, and length.

- Street Maintenance Management System (STREET) makes it easier to maintain public streets, including any road signs and storm drains. It also stores data on street lengths and widths, composition, and recurring problems. It can automatically generate work orders.

- Wastewater Collection Management System (WCMS) provides for the maintenance of underground sewers and storm-drain lines. Like CASS, it provides for downloading data from laptops, and correlating TV images with the collected reports.

- Water Distribution Management System (WDMS) provides for scheduling maintenance and field inspections of the city water system. It provides for inventories of the water mains, valves, hydrants, meters, and storage units.

All of the Hansen Software applications run as C/S systems, with Intel-based PCs running Windows 3.*x* as the front end, and ORACLE running on an IBM RS/6000, Data General minicomputer, or VAX as the back end. The applications can also interface to engineering and mapping systems such as AutoCAD and Intergraph to provide links to system maps and blueprints.

KIVA

KIVA Systems provides a series of applications designed to assist city administrators, planners, and community development directors in managing city development and growth. They include applications for tracking building permits, population growth and changes, land use, and citizen service requests. The KIVA applications are

- Building Permits and Inspection (BPI)
- Development Monitoring System
- General Permitting System
- Impact Forecasting (Growth Management)
- Land Information System
- Project Management System
- Request for Services
- Work Order Management System
- Pavement Management

The KIVA applications can be used individually or as part of an integrated city-management system. The application's license includes providing the source code to the user site. The applications are written entirely in ORACLE SQL and PL/SQL, so additional front ends can be created by using application development tools from Oracle Corp. or third-party vendors.

The majority of KIVA systems are on Unix clients running Open Look or Motif. Typical clients include workstations from SUN and Apollo, and IBM RS/6000s. The ORACLE server software usually runs on an IBM RS/6000-970, though any ORACLE server is supported. PCs can also be used as front ends by communicating to the server through the TCP/IP protocol. Some of the KIVA applications can also interface with an Intergraph server to provide mapping functions.

MapNET Voter Registration and Reprecincting

Ecotran Systems's MapNET Voter Registration and Reprecincting is similar to its MapNET Boundary Planning and Redistricting, which is used for the education market. It tracks voter registrations and automatically assigns voters to the correct precinct and voting location. It can also be used to redraw precinct lines, based on the population.

Ecotran also sells MapNET Vehicle Scheduling, which creates driver assignments and maintenance schedules for city vehicles.

The primary front end for the MapNET applications is based on OS/2; one based on MS-DOS is also available. The server is based on an Intel 80486 system running the OS/2 or NLM version of ORACLE. Both packages can also support an HP 9000 running HP/UX as the server.

Publishing

The publishing industry ranges from the major book publishing houses to the big magazines to the smallest literary journal or newsletter. Though it seems that this industry would be ripe for computerization, I could find only one ORACLE-based application for it. If you're an application developer looking for an uncrowded market, you might want to consider writing applications for the publishing industry.

IAMS Subscription Management

IAMS Subscription Management, from Orange Systems, is designed to track reader subscriptions for periodicals and newsletters. It keeps track of expiration dates and can automatically create renewal notices. It can also print invoices and mailing labels. In addition to the standard data fields (name, address, etc.), it supports an extensive array of user-definable fields that a publisher can use to track reader demographics and other information.

Orange Systems has a couple of related applications, including IAMS Convention and Seminar Management, IAMS Membership Management, and the IAMS Exhibition/Exhibitor Management. All provide similar functions for their respective industries.

The IAMS systems are written entirely in Oracle's SQL*Forms, so they run on any system ORACLE supports, in host or C/S mode. However, the systems the company most often sells consist of MS-DOS clients with ORACLE running on a Unix server.

Retail and Sales

There are two general subcategories of applications that fall under this category. The majority of sales applications support sales organizations through computerized client leads and contact lists. Others provide point-of-sale (POS) systems for use as the cash registers in a retail store. Most retail and sales systems are host-based, but a few also support the C/S architecture.

Action Now!

Wellington Systems, whose Manufacturing Inventory Management System I discussed earlier, also sells Action Now!, a contact management system for sales professionals. Action Now! tracks customer information from the first contact to the final sale, providing the salesperson with a way to maintain client lists and to follow-up client contacts. It also provides mail-merge functions so that contact letters can be automatically generated. Its Macintosh-based interface makes extensive use of pull-down menus and pre-defined pick lists of information to ensure that the data is accurate.

The Action Now! database server can run on any platform supported by ORACLE. The client software runs on a Macintosh. Wellington also sells a single-user version that runs both the client and server software on the same Macintosh system.

ATMS

ATMS (Automated Telephone Management System), from Automated Telephone Management Systems, is a package designed for telemarketing organizations. It includes automated dialing functions from the data screen, so the sales representative can simply dial the client's phone number by pressing a function key while the client record is displayed. It includes client-list management functions, an appointment scheduler, a survey module, and a collection

module. Customized versions are available for the insurance, telemarketing, credit collection, publishing, stock broker, and marketing industries.

ATMS runs in either host-based or C/S modes. The database runs on various IBM and Unix platforms, as well as under OS/2. The client systems run under MS-DOS.

Aurum-TeleTrak

In addition to its quality control application(Aurum-QualityTrak) and support application (Aurum-SupportTrak), both of which I discussed in the manufacturing section, Aurum sells two applications for sales departments. All four applications can be tied together to form an integrated manufacturing, marketing, and support system.

Aurum-TeleTrak is designed for use by inside salespeople whose primary contact with clients is via the telephone. Aurum-TeleTrak maintains client lists, contact information, sales-lead information, and demographic and statistical information on clients and potential clients. It can also automatically dial a client's number from the on-screen record. It can generate sales orders and can be integrated with a number of word processing packages to create mail-merge letters.

Aurum-SalesTrak is a similar application designed for use by outside salespeople. It can generate sales quotes and create appointment schedules in addition to its client tracking capabilities. The information can be downloaded to and updated from a laptop or portable computer carried by the salesperson for on-the-road use.

Like Aurum-QualityTrack and Aurum-SupportTrak, Aurum-TeleTrak and Aurum-SalesTrak run on the Unix versions of ORACLE, in multiuser host or C/S mode. The C/S front-end application requires Windows 3.*x,* or a Unix GUI such as Motif or Open Look.

SQL*TIME Sales Leads Management

Design Data Systems Corp. checks into this chapter a final time with its SQL*TIME Sales Leads Management. This system automates the client contact process for both inside and outside salespeople. It maintains client and sales lead lists, and can automatically generate letters and faxes to follow up on client contacts. It can also flag client records for follow-ups and automatically display them on the screen after a user-defined period. It includes sales forecasting capabilities, based on the information a salesperson enters about a client's rank, status, and probability of making a purchase. SQL*TIME Sales Lead Management is primarily aimed at the real-estate industry, though it can be used by any organization that relies on an active sales force and client contacts.

All of the SQL*TIME applications are programmed with ORACLE Tools, so they support any ORACLE platform in multiuser host or C/S mode. Design Data is currently moving its SQL*TIME applications to version 7.0 of ORACLE and the new releases of ORACLE Tools.

TotalSTORE

Post Software International (PSI) sells System To Organize the Retail Environment (STORE), a client/server POS system based on an ORACLE database server with a custom-written front-end package. TotalSTORE is actually an integrated set of PSI's STORE POS modules that are linked together into a complete retail cash register and sales administration system.

TotalSTORE provides for point-of-sale cash management, price management, price verification based on stock numbers, and layaway sales. It can also be used to automate a central cash office, and provides a number of administrative functions and supports. Its four primary modules are Item Database, Financial Database, Personnel Database, and Customer Database. Other included modules provide for stockroom and floor inventory management, purchase orders, payroll budgeting, employee scheduling, and raincheck management.

TotalSTORE can gather inventory data downloaded from hand-held inventory counting devices. It also has the ability to run in a distributed environment, where each store maintains its own database server, and all the servers update a central server on a predetermined schedule.

PSI sells TotalSTORE as a complete hardware and software system. The primary front end is a custom-written character-mode application that runs under Unix or OS/2. The database server can be any platform supported by ORACLE. Though ORACLE is the primary platform for the STORE applications, PSI can port it to any other SQL database server that uses ANSI SQL, such as Sybase SQL Server or IBM's various SQL RDBMSs.

Travel and Tourism

Though the big airline-ticketing systems pretty much have the travel agency market locked up, there's still a big opportunity for software developers in the rest of the travel industry, such as hotels and motels, tour groups, and cruises. Unfortunately, this also seems to be a market that database developers are overlooking; for example, I answered a question in a *PC Magazine* Advisor column about software for managing the front desk of a motel, and had a hard time finding a reasonably priced system. The few systems I was able to find were for the most part based on proprietary databases running on central hosts. I couldn't find a single C/S hotel/motel management system.

Because of this, I'm going to close this chapter with the only ORACLE-based C/S system oriented toward the travel industry, and a note to database developers. If you're a developer looking for a C/S market to get into, check out the many aspects of the travel and tourism industry. This industry is wide open for new computer systems.

Automobile Club Processing System

Automation has written Automobile Club Processing System (CPS) as an automation system for automobile clubs, primarily American Automobile Association (AAA) offices. CPS gives the automobile club manager the ability to track members and membership sales by product, agent, office, and special programs. It processes new memberships and renewals, and stores demographic information so that special promotions and programs can be targeted to the appropriate members. It also tracks emergency road service (ERS) usage, as well as any other special services and programs members take advantage of. The ERS module can automatically relate the location a member broke down at with the nearest ERS garage or service center for dispatching. A full set of management reports are available to assist in pricing existing and new services, or to track service usage patterns.

The CPS also supports POS (point-of-sale) functions for insurance, traveler's checks, and travel-related products. It supports the centralized collection of information from branch offices through a distributed database system.

Automobile Club Processing System is written entirely in ORACLE Tools, so it runs on any system supported by ORACLE. The majority of CPS systems run in host mode, though more and more club offices are investigating the C/S option so they can use the same PCs for accessing both the club membership system and the airline ticketing system.

10

ORACLE, Version 7.0

New Features and
Capabilities

Platforms, Present and
Future

Impact on Current Tools
and Applications

What's Still Missing?

N LATE 1991, ORACLE FORMALLY ANNOUNCED THAT IT WAS WORKING ON the long-awaited new version of its flagship RDBMS. The initial plan was that ORACLE, version 7.0, would be released by the end of 1992; however, the start of 1993 saw only a limited release of the VMS version. Versions for other platforms are currently scheduled to be released during mid- to late 1993, with the OS/2 and NetWare versions at the head of the list.

The new version represents a ground-up redesign of the ORACLE RDBMS. In the four years since the release of version 6.0, other RDBMS vendors have increased the state of the art, particularly when it comes to C/S and distributed database capabilities. Oracle's chief competition is the Unix-based Sybase SQL Server, which Microsoft ported to OS/2, and which Sybase Corp. has released in an NLM version. Sybase SQL Server brought many innovations to the C/S marketplace; the most important of these was moving more of the processing to the server through the use of stored procedures and triggers. The backing of Microsoft on the PC platforms led Sybase SQL Server to become the top-selling RDBMS for C/S use on LANs. While ORACLE remains the best-selling RDBMS, the company sees version 7.0 as its best hope for gaining dominance in the PC-based C/S market.

Oracle is also already talking about version 8.0; it anticipates releasing this version in 1995. Details were very sketchy at the time of this writing, but indications are that version 8.0 will continue the move toward better C/S and distributed processing capabilities. The fact that Oracle is discussing future generations of its RDBMS while in the process of releasing the next generation is a good indication that the company is serious about gaining the top spot in the C/S market.

New Features and Capabilities

The changes in version 7.0 are so numerous and extensive that most of Volume III of the *Database Administrator's Guide* is dedicated to listing them and describing them in brief. In most cases, the list of changes refers the reader back to the particular portions of Volumes I and II that contain full information on the new commands, parameters, or features. On the one hand, this makes it easier to find the important information quickly when you're upgrading to the new version. On the other, be prepared to keep all three volumes handy and spend a lot of time going back and forth between them until you're completely familiar with all the changed and new features.

There are changes made and commands added to ORACLE's SQL and PL/SQL command set to make it 100 percent compatible with the ANSI SQL Level 2 standard with Integrity Enhancements. The changes and additions are detailed in version 7.0's *SQL Language Reference* manual, which was unavailable for review at the time of this writing.

The release version will include the *Version 6 to Version 7 Migration Guide,* which is designed to ease the process of upgrading existing databases and servers. Unfortunately, a beta copy of this manual also wasn't available in time for inclusion in this book.

Note that the information in this chapter is based on late beta documentation provided by Oracle. Some of the changed features described here may not make the final version of the software, or they may work a bit differently than the documentation currently describes. New features may also be added to the release version that haven't been finalized yet and thus aren't documented, though this is unlikely. It's safe to assume that any changes at this late date will be relatively minor and won't significantly affect the final product.

Changed Terminology

Version 7.0 introduces some new terms that better describe existing features in version 6.0 and make it easier to understand the changed functionality in version 7.0:

- *database objects*   The number of items that fall under the umbrella term "database objects" has been expanded beyond the tables, views, and users it referred to in version 6.0. In version 7.0, database objects include tables, views, users, snapshots, roles (the Oracle term for user groups), profiles, procedures, packages, triggers, and integrity constraints.

- *co-located objects*   These are database objects that exist within a single database. This term and the next describe the difference between objects in a single database and those scattered about a distributed database system.

- *non–co-located objects*   These are database objects that reside in different databases, usually two or more distributed databases.

- *initialization parameters and parameter files*   In version 6.0, the only initialization parameter file was INIT.ORA, which is used to set the defaults for how the database server works. Version 7.0 introduces a number of other parameter files, which set up defaults for users or roles, in addition to those for the RDBMS. Because of this, Oracle has broadened the term to refer to any of the parameter files, not just the main database's.

- *schema*   In the RDBMS world, a schema is the structure of a particular database. Oracle has narrowed this description to refer to the database objects owned by a particular user. In version 6.0, no distinction was made between the user and the database's objects.

- *server process*   In version 6.0, these were known as shadow processes. In version 7.0, a server process is a task started by the RDBMS to handle one or more user requests. Server processes are multithreaded.

- *session*   This is a logical connection between a user and a database. Every user can have more than one session established, to more than one database, depending on the configuration of the databases involved. The term "user session" replaces the "user process" used in version 6.0.

- *shared SQL areas*   This is the new term for what version 6.0 referred to as context areas. A context area is a private memory buffer on the server where parsed SQL statements issued by a user are stored. When the user reissues the same SQL statement, the RDBMS discards the new one and uses the existing one to save time and processing overhead.

In version 7.0, the context areas are no longer private to a particular user; the RDBMS stores the parsed SQL statement in a common memory buffer, and uses the parsed statement instead of the newly issued statements, regardless of who issued them. Shared SQL areas greatly reduce the processing and memory overhead on the database server.

NOTE.   *For more information, see the section "Shared SQL Areas" in this chapter.*

Datatype Changes

Significant changes have been made to the datatypes in version 7.0, particularly to the ones that store characters or binary data. In version 6.0, CHAR and VARCHAR were synonymous; in version 7.0, they're quite different. CHAR, LONG, LONG RAW, RAW, and ROWID have been changed in version 7.0 as well. DATE and NUMBER remain the same in the new version. The following lists the new and changed data types:

- *CHAR*   This is now a fixed-length field, with a maximum length of 255 characters. In version 6.0, it was a variable-size field that would automatically grow to the maximum, depending on the number of characters stored in it. When the number of characters in a particular data item is less than the size of the CHAR field, ORACLE automatically fills in the rest of the field with spaces.

- *VARCHAR2*   This new datatype is the replacement for version 6.0's VARCHAR; it stores variable-length character data up to a maximum of 2,000 characters. VARCHAR2 fields store data without padding out the rest of the field with spaces.

- *VARCHAR*   This is now an alias for the VARCHAR2 datatype; however, Oracle warns that VARCHAR may change or disappear in future versions, so all references to VARCHAR should be updated to VARCHAR2.

- *RAW*   Like VARCHAR2, RAW can be expanded to a maximum of 2,000 characters or non-character bytes.

- *LONG* and *LONG RAW*   These has been expanded from the maximum of 64K characters in version 6.0 to 2GB in version 7.0, making them equivalent to the generic BLOB (binary large object) data type. This is a significant enhancement, making ORACLE capable of handling binary image data in multimedia applications. As in version 6.0, LONG stores strictly characters and LONG RAW stores characters or binary data.

- *ROWID*   Externally, ROWID appears the same; however, changes have been made in its internal storage to provide support for the new and changed datatypes, and to support more objects per table.

Functionality

The most significant enhancement made in version 7.0's functionality is the addition of full compliance with the ANSI SQL Level 2 standard with Integrity Enhancements. All referential integrity functions are now active and can be enabled or disabled as needed. ORACLE automatically enforces unique keys, and it can also activate delete cascades, which automatically delete child rows when the parent row is deleted.

Stored Procedures and Triggers

The second significant enhancement is the addition of stored procedures and triggers, features already found in Microsoft SQL Server and Sybase SQL Server. *Stored procedures* are SQL or PL/SQL procedures or functions that are compiled and stored with the database on the server. Instead of sending the entire procedure down the cable, the client application can simply call the stored procedure, which is then executed directly on the server. This helps to reduce network traffic, and also makes it easier to maintain applications, as the procedures are stored in one central place instead of in each different front-end application. Along with this, version 7.0 supports *triggers*, which are specialized stored procedures that are automatically executed whenever a user inserts, updates, or deletes data from a table. A trigger can provide additional referential integrity, or it can notify the DBA or user when a particular action is taken.

Version 7.0 adds another type of stored procedure, called a package. A *package* can consist of one or more procedures, functions, constants, or variables. It lets you call these components as a single unit, which means you don't have to call each one individually. One advantage to using a package is that global constants and variables can retain their current value between sessions, regardless of which user application calls it.

Distributed Database Options

Distributed database options are also enhanced in version 7.0. All DML operations can be used across databases (in version 6.0, only queries were allowed); this lets the user access remote databases as if they were local. To support this, version 7.0 now includes a two-phase commit mechanism, to ensure that a distributed transaction is successful across all affected databases before returning a successful completion code to the user application. If any one of the database transactions fails, the two-phase commit treats all the transactions as having failed and rolls the databases back to their original state.

The Snapshot Capability   In order to speed up processing, version 7.0 supports a snapshot capability. *Snapshots* let the application manually make a read-only copy of one or more rows from a remote database table on the local server. They are ideal for linking local data to a remote lookup table, and serve both to reduce network traffic and speed up lookup processing.

Global Naming   Another addition is *global naming*, which lets an application refer to any database it can access without having to know the location of the database. In version 6.0, the DBA had to create links between local and remote databases before the users could access them. Global naming eliminates this requirement. In order for global naming to work properly, every database in the system must have a unique name.

Finally, the distributed option reduces overhead at the local database by passing SQL statements without modification to the remote database. The SQL statements are optimized on the remote database, and only the results of the statement are passed back to the user application.

Backup and Recovery

Version 7.0's database backup and recovery options have been enhanced, primarily in the parallel processing mode. When a parallel database is running, version 7.0 keeps a separate transaction log for each database instance operating on the server. In both parallel and single-processor versions, the entire database no longer has to be taken off-line to perform a backup or restore; individual tables can be backed up while users continue to have access to other tables in the database. Tables that are in use won't be backed up on-line.

Version 7.0 also supports *mirrored transaction logs* (Oracle refers to these as on-line redo logs), which write multiple copies of the log to different locations at the same time, avoiding a single point of failure. Log checkpoints can now be based on time intervals instead of the number of transactions, and they can also be forced by the DBA.

Security

Security has been greatly enhanced and expanded in version 7.0. The most significant new feature is the addition of *roles*, Oracle's name for user groups. Users can be designated as part of a role, and security rights can be granted on a role basis. This simplifies the process of maintaining user privileges; when the DBA adds a new user to a group, the user automatically assumes the same privileges as the group. As in version 6.0, the DBA can still grant individual rights to users beyond those provided by their role.

To support this, version 7.0 adds a new SQL command: CREATE USER. CREATE USER simply adds a new user to the database security tables, without granting any rights. The DBA can then add a user to a role to give the user the appropriate security rights. The DBA can also assign individual rights to the new user. User security rights have been expanded to cover individual database objects, in addition to entire databases.

Version 7.0 has enhanced database auditing as well. The DBA can set up the auditing process to audit individual user actions, table accesses, and even the execution of particular SQL statements (including stored procedures). Table auditing is independent of view auditing, depending on how it is set up. A table accessed through a view can be audited on its own, the view can be audited, or both can be audited simultaneously. The audit log will note whether the table was accessed directly or through a view.

Version 7.0 now complies with the C2-level security standard established by the National Computer Security Center (NCSC). This means that version 7.0 can be used in government installations requiring confidential access to the contents of a database. An optional version, called Trusted ORACLE, will also be available at a future date; it complies with the top-secret NCSC restrictions defined in the higher, B1 level.

Performance

One of the biggest complaints about version 6.0 is that it's a resource hog on the server; the RDBMS uses a lot of memory for each user process (approximately 250K), and performance greatly suffers if there isn't sufficient memory. Version 7.0 improves on this by providing a multithreaded architecture, where multiple users can share a single process, reducing overhead on the server. Additional performance enhancements have also been achieved through changes in the RDBMS's internal code. Tests performed at the Ziff-Davis Labs and other industry publications on the beta version of 7.0 found ORACLE'S performance to be significantly better than version 6.0's.

Cost-Based Optimization

Version 7.0 supports cost-based SQL optimization, in addition to the rule-based optimization supported by version 6.0. *Cost-based optimization* examines the SQL statements and optimizes them based on how much processor time each execution takes. The execution plan is based on the statement's syntax, the indexes and clusters associated with the table, and any special instructions given to the optimizer. In addition, the optimizer can use database statistics that are stored in the data dictionary to enhance the optimization process. The statistics can be created with the new command, SQL ANALYZE.

Hashed Tables and Clusters

Performance is also enhanced through the use of hashed tables and clusters. Hashing is better than indexing for small tables that rarely change and are primarily used for lookups. A hashed table provides better performance than an indexed table when the query is sure to return one and only one row. *Clusters* are used to group the data in a table in the same area on the disk. This also serves to speed up access to the data in the table.

Shared SQL Areas

Shared SQL areas also enhance performance by retaining frequently used SQL statements in a common memory buffer on the server. This eliminates the need for the server to compile and optimize the same SQL statement when it's issued by multiple users. The first time the statement is issued, the server performs all the necessary steps to execute it. Subsequent occurrences of the same statement are discarded, and the server uses the shared statement to execute the new queries.

The TRUNCATE Command

Finally, SQL's TRUNCATE command has been added to remove all the data in a table quickly without changing or removing the structure of the table itself. TRUNCATE is better than DELETE for emptying tables that are used for temporary processing.

Administration

Database administration has been enhanced in a number of ways in version 7.0. Rollback segments are now more efficient; the DBA can specify individual rollback segments for each transaction, and the rollback segments can dynamically change size, depending on the amount of information currently being stored.

Resource limits can now be set based on individual users, which aids in tuning the database system by preventing unnecessary resource use. The DBA can set resource limits for CPU usage, logical I/O, idle time, connect time, and the number of open sessions and memory usage. They can also be set on a per-session basis. The DBA can set these limits globally, or through individual user or role profiles that automatically set the limits each time a user accesses the database. The ALTER SYSTEM command has been added to enable global resource limits, and to let the DBA set other configuration and tuning parameters for the entire RDBMS.

The Data Dictionary

The ORACLE data dictionary (or master system tables) has been completely revised for version 7.0. A number of version 6.0 data dictionary views are now obsolete, and 23 existing dictionary views have been changed to work with the new features in version 7.0. There are also 44 new dictionary views. A command file called CATALOG6.SQL is included to re-create the version 6.0 views in the version 7.0 data dictionary if you have routines that are dependent on them. The only difference is that version 6.0 views with the same name as those in version 7.0 have a "6" appended to the end of the view name.

In order to make a smooth migration from version 6.0 to version 7.0, a migration tool included in the package converts a version 6.0 database and database dictionary to the version 7.0 format. In addition, the DBA can specify that version 6.0 compatibility should be retained with the SET COMPATIBILITY command. This primarily affects the CHAR datatype and the CREATE TABLE statement, which would continue to function as they did in version 6.0.

Utilities: Changes in SQL*DBA and SQL*Loader

The most changed utility in version 7.0 is SQL*DBA, the interactive SQL query and administration tool. The new version now has a character-mode menu-driven interface, with pull-down menus that lead the user through the various operations. Figure 10.1 shows SQL*DBA's new menu-driven interface.

SQL*DBA

In SQL*DBA, menu items can now be chosen with the keyboard or with a mouse. The menu items include

- *Session*   The options here let the user connect to or disconnect from a database. This item also offers a command-line window, where individual SQL statements can be entered.

Figure 10.1

Version 7.0's SQL*DBA has a new menu-driven interface that makes it easier to access and administrate the database server.

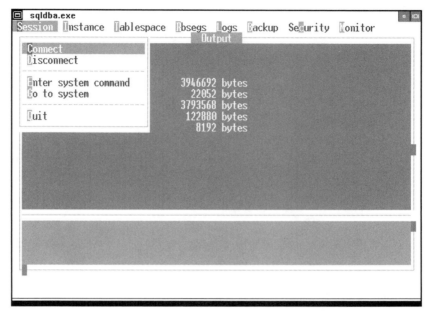

- *Instance*   The options in this submenu are primarily for database administration. They let the DBA start up and shut down the server, mount databases, and force log-file checkpoints. Additional options provide database configuration control and let the DBA kill a user session.

- *Tablespace*   This menu makes it easy to create, drop, and manage data tables. You can see the new menus in Figure 10.2.

- *Rbsegs*   This menu lets the DBA control the database hard-disk storage parameters.

- *Logs*   The options here guide the DBA through the process of creating and managing groups. They also let the DBA enable and disable database threads of execution, and turn the log-file mirroring on and off. Figure 10.3 shows the various options in the Logs menu.

- *Backup*   This menu controls both table and database backups and recovery.

- *Security*   This menu controls the creation and management of users, and the granting of appropriate rights. It also lets the DBA create user and group profiles. The various menu items are shown in Figure 10.4.

Figure 10.2

The SQL*DBA Tablespace menu makes it easier to manage tables in a database.

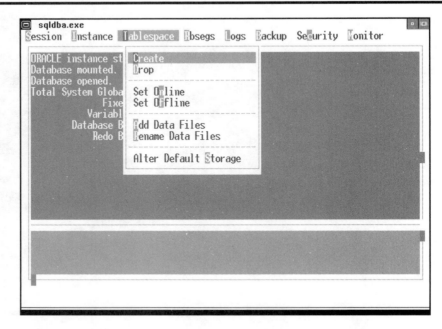

Figure 10.3

The Logs menu guides the DBA through the process of creating and managing groups, threads, and database logs.

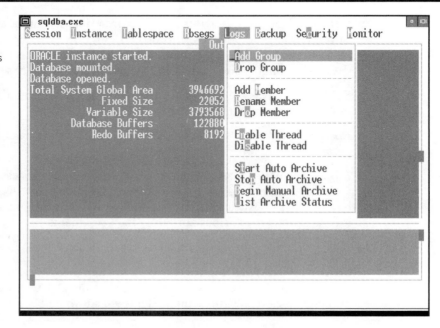

Figure 10.4

The DBA can use the Security menu to control user access to the database.

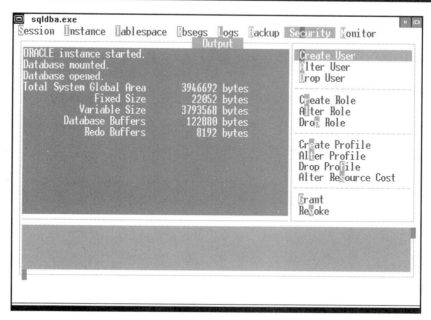

- *Monitor*   The options here bring up the various database monitors. Figure 10.5 shows the windowed command line. The DBA can use it to enter SQL statements directly, without having to go through the menus. It can also be used to run SQL statements stored in a text file.

Database Monitors

The database monitors have been completely revamped with new features, and new monitors have been added. SQL*DBA now supports the following types:

- *File I/O monitor*   This monitor lets the DBA track the read and write activity on each file in the database.

- *Latch monitor*   This monitor tracks the latches (or locks) on shared data structures in the System Global Area (SGA).

- *Lock monitor*   This shows the DBA which database objects are currently locked.

- *Process monitor*   This monitor shows the status of all user and background processes in the database.

Figure 10.5

SQL statements can also be entered directly through the pop-up command windows.

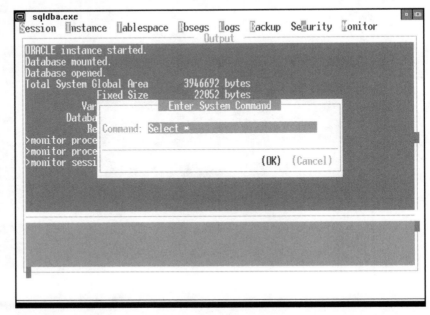

- *Rollback-segment monitor* The DBA can use this monitor to track the current size and status of the log-file rollback segments.

- *Session monitor* This provides information and statistics on each user session.

- *Statistics monitor* This is probably the most important monitor for fine-tuning the system; it shows the amount of memory and CPU usage by the database users, the current information on the redo (rollback) logs, the performance of the database lock queues, and the performance of the I/O cache. Figure 10.6 shows the various items monitored in the statistics monitor.

- *System I/O distribution monitor* This monitor shows the percentage of total I/O activity for each process in the system.

- *Table access monitor* This lets the DBA track which tables are in use, and who's using them.

A welcome feature is one that now lets you run multiple monitors at the same time, each in its own window.

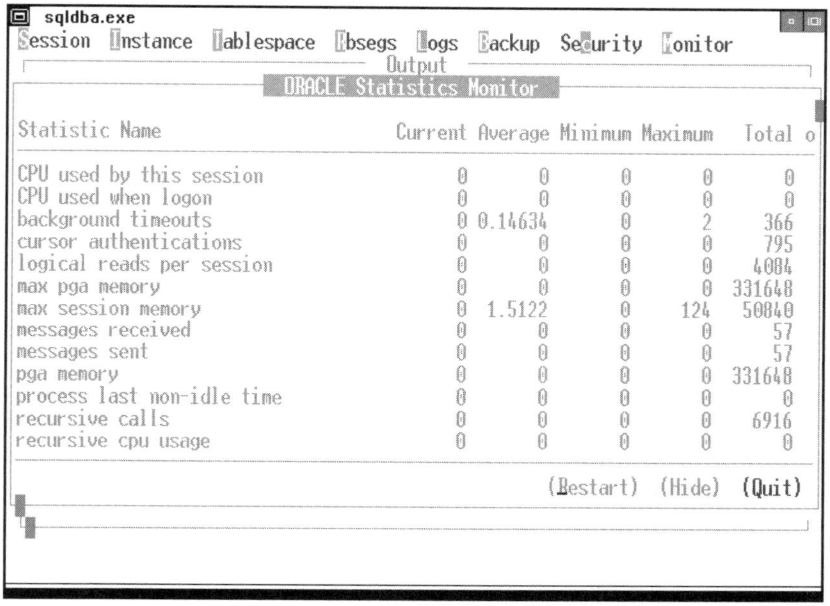

Figure 10.6

The statistics monitor lets you keep an eye on the overall system performance.

```
sqldba.exe
 Session  Instance  Tablespace  Rbsegs  Logs  Backup  Security  Monitor
                              Output
                     ORACLE Statistics Monitor

 Statistic Name              Current Average Minimum Maximum   Total o

 CPU used by this session          0        0       0       0       0
 CPU used when logon               0        0       0       0       0
 background timeouts               0 0.14634       0       2     366
 cursor authentications            0        0       0       0     795
 logical reads per session         0        0       0       0    4084
 max pga memory                    0        0       0       0  331648
 max session memory                0   1.5122       0     124   50840
 messages received                 0        0       0       0      57
 messages sent                     0        0       0       0      57
 pga memory                        0        0       0       0  331648
 process last non-idle time        0        0       0       0       0
 recursive calls                   0        0       0       0    6916
 recursive cpu usage               0        0       0       0       0

                                       (Restart)  (Hide)  (Quit)
```

New Commands and Functions

Several new commands and functions have been added to SQL*DBA as well. The DBA can now use the STARTUP RESTRICTED command to limit database access to certain users. ALTER SYSTEM can be used to start and stop restricted access on the fly. As I mentioned previously, the KILL SESSION command lets the DBA terminate a user's session. And finally, the DESCRIBE command can now be used from SQL*DBA to get information on tables, views, and stored procedures.

Those who prefer the interactive command line that the version 6.0 SQL*DBA provided can still access it by starting SQL*DBA with LMODE=Y on the command line. Note, though, that the monitors are unavailable when you run SQL*DBA in version 6.0 compatibility mode.

SQL*Loader

The data import and export utility has been updated to support all the database objects in version 7.0. SQL*Loader (the bulk-data loading utility) has been enhanced to load data directly into the database without having to go through the RDBMS's SQL processing. This enhancement significantly improves data loading performance.

Miscellaneous Other Changes

View handling has been improved in version 7.0. In version 6.0, you had to create every table referenced by a view prior to creating the view. This is no longer the case in version 7.0. However, the view can't be accessed until all the underlying tables exist. Views can also be dropped and re-created with one new command: CREATE OR ALTER VIEW. When this command is used, existing user rights for the original view are carried over to the new one.

Version 7.0 supports larger control files than did version 6.0; the exact size depends on the operating system under which the RDBMS is running. The new limits will be detailed in the appropriate database manuals for each operating system. The maximum number of files in the database has been increased from version 6.0's limit of 255 to at least 1,022. Again, more can be created depending on the operating system.

Data storage has been optimized, and version 7.0's databases will take up less disk space than the equivalent version 6.0 databases. And finally, the existing error messages have been updated, and new error messages added to support all the new features in version 7.0.

Platforms, Present and Future

Oracle has traditionally released new versions of its RDBMS for the VAX/VMS platform first, as this was where the product was originally developed, and it remains ORACLE's largest installed base. Version 7.0 hasn't changed that tradition; at the time of this writing, Oracle had released a limited number of VMS versions to its largest customer sites. The general release of the VMS version was scheduled to occur by May 1, 1993.

The SCO Xenix and OS/2 2.0 versions will be the next ones released, followed by the NLM version. Current plans are for these versions to go on sale by the end of the third quarter of 1993. Various other Unix versions will follow after that, and the mainframe VM and MVS versions will be the last ones released.

Oracle originally announced that it wouldn't be releasing a PC-DOS or MS-DOS version of 7.0, but customer outrage forced it to retract the decision. However, no firm decision had been made one way or the other at the time of this writing, so there's no scheduled release date for the DOS version.

Oracle has announced that it is also preparing a version for Microsoft Windows NT, to be released concurrently with or shortly after this operating system. Microsoft originally intended to release Windows NT at Spring Comdex in May 1993; however, current industry information indicates that this may be delayed to at least July or August 1993.

Impact on Current Tools and Applications

Version 7.0 will have a significant impact on existing third-party front ends, toolkits, and applications, and will in all likelihood "break" most of them. Third-party vendors have to update their products to support the new version. At this time, only Oracle itself and Powersoft have announced new versions of their application development tools.

Version 7.0 will have the greatest impact on custom applications. Developers of these applications should upgrade to the new versions of the ORACLE Tools package (or whatever toolkit they've used) as soon as they are available.

Upgrading a database server is like upgrading a critical computer's operating system. Potential users would be wise to plan the upgrade carefully, and not just install the new version on every existing server the day it arrives. This is one area where PC support personnel can learn a valuable lesson from the minicomputer and mainframe system programmers. These folks know that upgrading a major system shouldn't be done casually, without extensive testing on a noncritical system.

The best course of action is to install the upgrade on a backup server and test it with copies of existing databases to make sure it imports the data correctly and that the data can be accessed. The backup/test server should then be used as the foundation for testing and updating existing applications, or creating new applications. When the testing is complete, and the system support technicians are confident that everything is functioning correctly, the new version can be installed on existing systems.

The upgrade process should be done on a server-by-server basis. Even if everything checked out 100 percent during the testing phase, it isn't wise to upgrade every server at once. Do it one server at a time, and make sure the upgraded server is functioning properly before upgrading the next one. That way, if something goes wrong, it will be easier to trace the cause to the most recently upgraded server, instead of having to search through a number of servers to find the one causing the problem.

What's Still Missing?

While version 7.0 is a significant upgrade, there are still some features missing. In spite of improved memory management that provides for more users in the same amount of RAM, version 7.0 is still a memory resource hog compared with other C/S database servers available. Cutting down its memory usage would require a complete rewrite of the underlying database engine and operating-system interface modules. ORACLE users can only hope that version 8.0 will correct this problem.

The distributed database features in version 7.0 represent a significant enhancement over both version 6.0 and other RDBMSs. However, they've not yet had a significant testing under real-world conditions, so it remains to be seen whether they can be used to create a functioning distributed system.

Otherwise, version 7.0 provides the majority of features users and potential users have been asking for. The addition of stored procedures and triggers makes it the technological equal of its closest competitor, and keeps it in the running for the top spot in the C/S market. The new distributed database capabilities have the potential to make it the leader in the move to expanded database access.

Whether you're sticking with version 6.0 of ORACLE for the foreseeable future, or planing your upgrade to version 7.0, I hope you've found this book a help in getting the most out of one of the premier RDBMSs available.

Chart of Products and Platforms

	DOS	Windows	OS/2	Macintosh	Unix (character-mode)	Unix (GUI)	VAX/VMS	MVS VM
Chapter 4								
ORACLE Tools	x		x	x	x	x	x	x
SQL Windows		x						
PowerBuilder		x						
ObjectVision		x	x					
Object/1		x	x					
Chapter 5								
Paradox SQL Link	x	x						
Superbase		x						
R:Base for Vanguard	x		x					
DataEase	x	x	x					
Q&A	x							
Lotus 1-2-3	x	x	x					
Advanced Revelation	x				x			
Q&E Database Editor family		x	x					
Clarion Professional	x							
Focus	x		x		x			
Wingz		x	x	x		x		
Chapter 6								
Quest		x						
R&R Report Writer for ORACLE	x	x			x			

	DOS	Windows	OS/2	Macintosh	Unix (character-mode)	Unix (GUI)	VAX/VMS	MVS VM
Impromptu		x		x				
ClearAccess		x						
DataPivot and DataPrism		x		x				
Personal Access		x		x				
ORACLE Card		x		x				
Chapter 7								
Forest & Trees	x	x						
LightShip		x						
Command Center	x	x		x	x		x	x
GQL		x		x		x		
Approach for Windows		x						
Intelligent Query (IQ)	x		x		x		x	
Chapter 8								
EXSYS Professional	x	x	x		x	x	x	
KBMS	x	x	x		x	x	x	x
KnowledgePro Windows		x						
NEXPERT Object					x			
ERwin/ERX		x		x		x		
Adaptfile Document Image Processing System	x							
EasyFile 3000 and ExpressFile 7000		x			x			
Feith Document Database		x						

	DOS	Windows	OS/2	Macintosh	Unix (character-mode)	Unix (GUI)	VAX/VMS	MVS VM
METAMORPH	x	x		x	x		x	
PRC Technical Document Management System	x		x		x		x	
PRC's Image Management System	x	x	x	x	x	x	x	
TOPIC	x		x	x	x		x	
Chapter 9								
ALCIE IV	x		x	x	x	x	x	x
Axtell Fixed Asset	x		x	x	x	x	x	x
Banner Finance System	x	x	x		x			
MT/PSMS		x					x	
Recovery 1			x		x		x	
SQL*TIME Financials	x		x	x	x	x	x	x
CIID				x	x		x	
JIT Distribution System	x		x	x	x			
SQL*TIME Distribution	x		x	x	x	x	x	x
Conference Services	x		x				x	
Housing Information Services	x		x				x	
MapNET Boundary Planning and Redistricting	x		x					
RIMS				x				
STAR_BASE	x			x	x			
ARIS	x		x			x	x	

	DOS	Windows	OS/2	Macintosh	Unix (character-mode)	Unix (GUI)	VAX/VMS	MVS VM
CLIN.GCP	x		x			x	x	
CLIN.DB	x		x			x	x	
PCRS	x		x				x	
PILLS	x		x			x	x	
CLINTROL			x		x		x	
DSI Financial/Accounting System	x		x	x	x	x	x	x
Patient Care Management System	x				x			
VITALNET	x							
EMPIRE/SQL	x		x	x	x	x	x	x
PS/HRMS		x						
Aurum-QualityTrak		x				x		
Aurum-SupportTrak		x				x		
CIIM				x				
CIFAS				x				
EMIS family		x						
Impression	x				x			
ICIM	x		x	x	x	x	x	x
Just-in-Time Manufacturing System	x		x	x	x			
JIT Graphical User Interface		x						
Manufacturing Inventory Management System				x				
CASS (various)	x							

	DOS	Windows	OS/2	Macintosh	Unix (character-mode)	Unix (GUI)	VAX/VMS	MVS VM
EDMS, GDMS, STREET, WCMS, WDMS		x						
KIVA (various)	x					x		
MapNET Voter Registration and Reprecincting	x		x					
IAMS Subscription Management System	x		x	x	x	x	x	x
Action Now!				x				
ATMS	x							
Aurum-TeleTrak		x				x		
Aurum-SalesTrak		x				x		
SQL*TIME Sales Leads Management	x		x	x	x	x	x	x
TotalSTORE			x		x			
Automobile Club Processing System	x		x	x	x	x	x	x

Listing of Vendor Information

Adaptive Information Systems, Inc.
24461 Ridge Route Dr.
Laguna Hills, CA 92653
(714) 587-9077
Products: AdaptFile Document Image Processing System

Andyne Computing, Ltd.
552 Princess St.
Second Floor
Kingston, Ontario, Canada
(613) 548-4355
Products: GQL

Applied Collegiate Systems Division
1133 Corporate Dr.
Farmington, NY 14425
(716) 924-7121
Products: Conference Services, Housing Information System

Approach Software Corp.
311 Penobscot Dr.
Redwood City, CA 94063
(415) 306-7890
Products: Approach for Windows

Aurum Software, Inc.
5201 Great America Pkwy.
Suite 240
Santa Clara, CA 95054
(408) 562-6370
Products: Aurum-QualityTrak, Aurum-SalesTrak, Aurum-SupportTrak,
Aurum-TeleTrak

Automated Telephone Management Systems, Inc.
1111 International Pkwy.
Suite 230
Richardson, TX 75081
(214) 669-2333
Products: ATMS (Automated Telephone Management System)

Automation, Inc.
10703 J St.
Omaha, NE 68127
(402) 339-9500
Products: Automobile Club Processing System

Avalon Software, Inc.
3716 E. Columbia
Suite 120
Tucson, AZ 85714
(602) 790-4214
Products: Computer Interactive Financial Accounting System (CIFAS), Computer Interactive Integrated Distribution (CIID), Computer Interactive Integrated Manufacturing (CIIM)

Axtell Development Corp.
4102 W. Hayward Ave.
Phoenix, AZ 85051
(602) 255-0508
Products: Axtell Fixed Assets

Borland International, Inc.
P.O. Box 660001
1800 Green Hills Rd.
Scotts Valley, CA 95066-0001
(408) 438-8400
Products: ObjectVision, ObjectVision SQL Connection, Paradox, Paradox SQL Link

Brio Technology, Inc.
444 Castro St.
Suite 700
Mountain View, CA 94041
(415) 961-4110
Products: DataPivot, DataPivot for Windows, DataPrism, DataPrism for Windows

Cadre Technologies, Inc.
222 Richmond St.
Providence, RI 02903
(401) 351-5950
Products: Cadre DB Designer, Teamwork CASE tools

C D Data Corp.
2887 22nd Ave. North
St. Petersburg, FL 33713
(813) 323-2277
Products: ALCIE IV

Century Consultants, Ltd.
300 Main St.
Lakewood, NJ 08701
(908) 363-9300
Products: STAR_BASE

Clarion Software, Inc.
150 E. Sample Rd.
Pompano Beach, FL 33064
(305) 785-4555
Products: Clarion Professional Developer

ClearAccess Corp.
200 W. Lowe St.
Fairfield, IA 52556
(515) 472-7077
Products: ClearAccess

Clinical Information Services, Inc.
15 Bank St.
Stamford, CT 06901
(203) 964-8317
Products: ARIS (Adverse Reaction Information System), CLIN.GCP (Clinical Trial Management System), PCRS (Product Complaint Report System), PILLS (Package Insert Labeling & Logistics System)

Cognos Corp.
67 S. Bedford St.
Burlington, MA 01803
(617) 229-6600
Products: Impromptu

Computer Financial Corp.
222 Northfield Rd.
Suite 200
Northfield, IL 60093
(708) 441-0410
Products: CLINTROL

Concentric Data Systems, Inc.
110 Turnpike Rd.
Westborough, MA 01581
(508) 366-1122
Products: R&R Report Writer for ORACLE

Critikon, Inc. (A Johnson & Johnson Company)
4110 George Rd.
Tampa, FL 33634
(813) 887-2000
Products: VITALNET System

DataEase International, Inc.
7 Cambridge Dr.
Trumbull, CT 06611
(203) 374-8000
Products: DataEase, DataEase Express for Windows, DataEase for Windows,
DataEase SQL Connect

DeLair Systems, Inc.
2639 N. 33rd Ave.
Phoenix, AZ 85009
(602) 269-8373
Products: DSI Financial/Accounting System, DSI Patient Accounting/Receivables Management

Design Data Systems Corp.
11701 S. Belcher Rd.
Suite 105
Largo, FL 34643
(813) 539-1077
Products: SQL*TIME Distribution, SQL*TIME Financials, SQL*TIME Inventory, SQL*TIME Order Entry, SQL*TIME Purchase Order, SQL*TIME Sales Leads Management

Digital Equipment Corp. (DEC)
146 Main St.
Maynard, MA 01754-2571
(508) 493-5111
Products: DECNet, Rdb/VMS, ULTRIX, VAX/VMS; DECStation, MicroVAX, MiniVAX, and VAX computer systems

DocuPoint, Inc.
2701 Bayview Dr.
Fremont, CA 94538
(510) 770-1189
Products: EasyFile 3000, ExpressFile 7000

Ecotran Systems, Inc.
21111 Chagrin Blvd.
Beachwood, OH 44122
(216) 991-9000
Products: MapNet Boundary Planning and Redistricting, MapNet Bus Routing,
MapNet Vehicle Scheduling, MapNet Voter Registration and Reprecincting

ESI Technologies, Inc.
237 Main St.
Seventh Floor
Buffalo, NY 14203-2702
(716) 852-8000
Products: EMIS series of manufacturing applications (15 in all)

EXSYS, Inc.
1720 Louisiana Blvd. NE
Suite 312
Albuquerque, NM 87110
(505) 256-8356
Products: EXSYS Professional

Eyring Corp.
1455 West 820 North
Provo, UT 84601
(801) 375-2434
Products: Impression

First Data Resources
One Lake Point Plaza
4235 South Stream Blvd.
Suite 180
Charlotte, NC 28217
(704) 357-6041
Products: Recovery 1

Feith Systems and Software, Inc.
425 Maryland Dr.
Fort Washington, PA 19034
(215) 646-8000
Products: Feith Document Database

Fibronics International, Inc.
One Lowell Research Center
847 Rogers St.
Lowell, MA 01852
(508) 937-1600
Products: KNET

Fusion Systems Group, Ltd.
225 Broadway
24th Floor
New York, NY 10007
(212) 285-8001
Products: Wingz DataLink for Oracle, Wingz DataLink for Sybase

Gupta Corp.
1060 Marsh Rd.
Menlo Park, CA 94025
(415) 321-9500
Products: Quest, SQLBase Server, SQLWindows

Hansen Information Technologies
1745 Markston Rd.
Sacramento, CA 95825
(916) 921-0883
Products: EDMS, GDMS, STREET, WCMS, WDMS

Hewlett-Packard Co.
3000 Hanover St.
Palo Alto, CA 94304
(415) 857-1501
Products: AllBase/4GL, AllBase/Query, AllBase/SQL, HP-UX, MPE/XL;
Apollo workstations, HP 3000- and HP 9000-series minicomputers

Humanic Design Corp.
1200 MacArthur Blvd.
Mahwah, NJ 07430
(201) 825-8887
Products: EMPIRE/SQL

IBM Corp.
Old Orchard Rd.
Armonk, NY 10504
(914) 765-1900
Products: AIX, DB2, DOS/VSE, MVS/XA, OS/2 2.0, OS/2 2.0 ES Database
Manager, PC-DOS, SQL/DS, SQL/400; PCs, minicomputers, and mainframes

Information Builders, Inc.
1250 Broadway
New York, NY 10001
(212) 736-4433
Products: EDA/SQL, Focus, PC/Focus

Informix Software, Inc.
4100 Bohannon Dr.
Menlo Park, CA 94025
(415) 926-6300
Products: INFORMIX-NET, INFORMIX-OnLine, INFORMIX-OnLine/Se-
cure, INFORMIX-SE, INFORMIX-STAR, Wingz, Wingz Datalinks

Ingres Corp.
P.O. Box 4026
1080 Marina Village Pkwy.
Alameda, CA 94501-1095
(510) 769-1400
Products: INGRES/Gateway, INGRES/Net, INGRES Server, INGRES/Star,
INGRES/Tools

Interlink Computer Sciences, Inc.
47370 Fremont Blvd.
Fremont, CA 94538
(510) 657-9800
Products: Interlink Application Gateway - TCPaccess

IQ Software Corp.
3295 River Exchange Dr.
Suite 550
Norcross, GA 30092
(404) 446-8880
Products: Intelligent Query (IQ) Access

Jostens Learning Corp.
6170 Cornerstone Ct. East
Suite 300
San Diego, CA 92121
(619) 587-0087
Products: Renaissance Instructional Management System (RIMS)

Just In Time Enterprise Systems, Inc.
1705 S. Capital Of Texas Hwy.
Suite 400
Austin, TX 78746
(512) 328-1241
Products: JIT Discrete Manufacturing System, JIT Distribution System, JIT
Finance System, The JIT Graphical User Interface, JIT Manufacturing System

KIVA Systems
5525 South 900 East
Suite 325
Salt Lake City, UT 84117
(801) 261-2617
Products: KIVA series of public sector/government applications (nine in all)

Knowledge Garden, Inc.
Stony Brook Technology Park
12-8 Technology Dr.
Setauket, NY 11733
(516) 246-5400
Products: KnowledgePro Windows

Logic Works, Inc.
214 Carnegie Ctr.
Suite 112
Princeton, NJ 08540
(609) 243-0088
Products: ERwin/DBF, ERwin/ERX, ERwin/SQL

Lotus Development Corp.
55 Cambridge Pkwy.
Cambridge, MA 02142
(617) 577-8500
Products: DataLens Driver for SQL Server, Lotus 1-2-3

Management Technologies, Inc.
3331 W. Big Beaver
Suite 105
Troy, MI 48084
(313) 643-1915
Products: MT/PSMS

Metasystems, Inc.
3645 Warrensville Center Rd.
Suite 328
Shaker Heights, OH 44122
(216) 561-9111
Products: Interactive Computer Integrated Manufacturing (ICIM)

Micro Data Base Systems, Inc.
Two Executive Dr.
P.O. Box 6089
Lafayette, IN 47905-6089
(317) 447-1122
Products: GURU, KnowledgeMan, MDBS IV, Object/1

Microrim, Inc.
15395 S.E. 30th Pl.
Bellevue, WA 98007
(206) 649-9500
Products: R:BASE, R:BASE for Vanguard

Microsoft Corp.
One Microsoft Way
Redmond, WA 98052-6339
(206) 882-8080
Products: Microsoft C 7.0, Microsoft Excel, Microsoft LAN Manager, Microsoft SQL Server, Microsoft Windows NT, Microsoft Windows 3.1, Microsoft Visual BASIC, MS-DOS 5.0

NCR Corp.
2700 Snelling Ave. North
St. Paul, MN 55113
(612) 638-7777
Products: Comten System 3000, Comten TCP/IP, MCAM

Neuron Data, Inc.
156 University Ave.
Palo Alto, CA 94301
(415) 321-4488
Products: NEXPERT Object

Novell, Inc.
122 East 1700 South
Provo, UT 84606-6914
(801) 429-7000
Products: NetWare 3.11, NetWare SQL, NetWare BTrieve

Oracle Corp.
500 Oracle Pkwy.
Redwood Shores, CA 94065
(415) 506-7000
Products: ORACLE Card, Oracle for 1-2-3 DataLens, ORACLE Server 6.0
and 7.0, SQL*Forms, SQL*Menu, SQL*Plus, SQL*ReportWriter, SQL*Text-
Retrieval

Orange Systems
13 Firstfield Rd.
Gaithersburg, MD 20878
(301) 840-2220
Products: IAMS Convention and Seminar Management, IAMS Exhibition/
Exhibitor Management, IAMS Subscription Management

Pacer Software, Inc.
1900 W. Park Dr.
Suite 280
Westborough, MA 01581
(508) 898-3300
Products: DAL Server for UNIX

PeopleSoft, Inc.
1331 N. California Blvd.
Suite 400
Walnut Creek, CA 94596
(510) 946-9460
Products: PS/HRMS

Pilot Software, Inc.
40 Broad St.
Boston, MA 02109
(617) 350-7035
Products: Command Center, LightShip, LightShip Lens

Pioneer Software, Inc.
5540 Centerview Dr.
Suite 324
Raleigh, NC 27606
(919) 859-2220
Products: Q&E Database Editor, Q&E Database Library, Q&E DataLink/
OV, Q&E DataLink/VB

Powersoft Corp.
70 Blanchard Rd.
Burlington, MA 01803
(617) 229-2200
Products: PowerBuilder DB2 Interface, PowerBuilder for Windows, Power-
Builder XDB Interface

PRC, Inc.
1500 Planning Research Dr.
McLean, VA 22102
(703) 556-1000
Products: PRC Image Management System, PRC Technical Document Management System

PSI, Inc.
14101 U.S. Hwy. 1
Youngsville, NC 27596
(919) 556-6721
Products: KAP, SpecialSTORE, SuperSTORE, TotalSTORE

Q. S., Inc.
P.O. Box 847
Nationsbank Plaza
Suite 1106
Greenville, SC 29602
(803) 232-2666
Products: Patient Care Management System (PCMS)

Revelation Technologies, Inc.
181 Harbor Dr.
Stamford, CT 06902
(203) 973-1000
Products: Advanced Revelation, DB2 Bond, ORACLE Server Bond, SQL
Server Bond

RJN Computer Services, Inc.
202 W. Front St.
Wheaton, IL 60187
(708) 682-4801
Products: CASS WORKS SEWER, CASS WORKS STORMWATER, CASS
WORKS WATER

Sequent Computer Systems, Inc.
15450 S.W. Koll Pkwy.
Beaverton, OR 97006-6063
(503) 626-5700
Products: Symmetry series multiprocessor superservers

ShareBase Corp. (Subsidiary Of Teradata Corp.)
2055A Logic Dr.
San Jose, CA 95124
(408) 369-5500
Products: SQL Server/8000 series multiprocessor superservers

Software Publishing Corp. (SPC)
3165 Kifer Rd.
P.O. Box 54983
Santa Clara, CA 95056-0983
(408) 986-8000
Products: Superbase 4, Superbase SQL Library

Spinnaker Software Corp.
201 Broadway
6th Floor
Cambridge, MA 02139-1901
(617) 494-1200
Products: Personal Access, PLUS

Sybase, Inc.
6475 Christie Ave.
Emeryville, CA 94608
(510) 596-3500
Products: Sybase SQL Server

Symantec Corp.
10201 Torre Ave.
Cupertino, CA 95014-2132
(408) 253-9600
Products: Q&A

Systems & Computer Technology Corp. (SCT)
Four Country View Rd.
Malvern, PA 19355
(215) 647-5930
Products: Banner Finance System

Thunderstone Software
11115 Edgewater Dr.
Cleveland, OH 44102
(216) 631-8544
Products: METABOOK, METAMORPH, 3DB

Trinzic Corp.
138 Technology Dr.
Waltham, MA 02254-9748
(617) 891-6500
Products: Forest & Trees, Forest & Trees for Windows, KBMS

Verity, Inc.
1550 Plymouth St.
Mountain View, CA 94043-1230
(415) 960-7600
Products: TOPIC, TOPIC REAL-TIME, TOPIC SDK

Wellington Systems, Inc.
40 Richards Ave.
Norwalk, CT 06854
(203) 866-4900
Products: Action Now!, Manufacturing Inventory Management System

XDB Systems, Inc.
14700 Sweitzer Ln.
Laurel, MD 20707-2921
(301) 317-6800
Products: XDB-LINK for DB2, XDB-Server, XDB-Workbench for DB2

GLOSSARY

ANSI SQL Level 2 Integrity addendum   The portion of the ANSI SQL Level 2 standard document that describes how referential integrity should be implemented.

ANSI SQL Level 2 with Integrity Enhancements   The current American National Standards Institute (ANSI) standard for SQL, issued in 1989. Sometimes referred to as the ANSI SQL-89 standard, it replaced the Level 1 version, the ANSI SQL-86 standard.

application programming interface (API)   The standard programming procedures, functions, and calls provided by an application or operating system. An application developer uses the API to interface with the parent application or operating system, instead of having to write custom procedures.

application prototyping utility   A type of code generator that assists programmers in designing and testing the screens, reports, etc. for an application before they write the program code. The utility may also contain a code generator, or it may just outline the final application by using skeleton code.

asymmetrical multiprocessing   A multiprocessing system in which each CPU is responsible for a different task. For example, one CPU handles the operating system while another runs the DBMS. In some asymmetrical multiprocessing systems, certain tasks, such as system interrupts, are always handled by the same CPU.

back end   A common term for the database server or application in a client/server system.

bridge   A hardware/software combination connecting two LANs using the same or different topologies and the same network protocol. A bridge simply combines two or more smaller LANs into one large LAN and passes all network traffic to both parts. Some modern bridges can also filter network traffic or route different protocols between the individual LANs. Bridges that also have these routing features are usually referred to as bridge/routers or brouters.

Bus   The part or subsystem of a computer that connects peripherals to the main CPU. It is also known as the data bus.

business rules   SQL statements and commands that enforce user-specified rules for the values of one or more columns in a database. A business rule's values are usually more restrictive than is the domain of the column. For example, the domain of a salary column may be "$0 to $99,000", but the business rule may restrict the maximum value according to each employee's job classification.

character coding   A standard method of translating characters such as alphabetical letters, numbers, and symbols into a binary code for storage and manipulation on a computer. The two current standards are ASCII and EBCDIC.

client/server database   A database system in which the database engine and database applications reside on separate intelligent computers that communicate with each other through a network. In this way, the processing power is split between the two CPUs. The user's workstation is the client, and the DBMS runs on the server.

clustered index   A method of indexing a database used by some DBMS vendors, in which the data in a table is physically arranged on the disk so it closely matches the index order. It reduces the delays when accessing data from large tables. ORACLE implements clustered indexes by physically prejoining two or more tables on the disk.

clustering   The linking of two or more DEC VAX/VMS systems so they can automatically share CPUs and resources. The linked computers appear as one system to users.

coaxial cable   An electrical networking cable that has an insulated center core surrounded by an exterior braid and additional layers of insulation. The cabling used for cable TV systems is a familiar example.

code generator   An application development tool (usually menu-driven) with which users can create DBMS applications without writing program code. The user lays out the steps the application should take, and the code generator writes the code that carries out those steps.

co-located object   The ORACLE, version 7.0, term for a database object that exists within a single database.

computer-aided system engineering (CASE)   A class of application development toolkits that help system engineers design and develop complex applications.

cost-based optimization   An advanced method of optimizing SQL statements before execution. In a cost-based system, the DBMS analyzes the

SQL statement against the amount of CPU time, resources, and available access methods—indexes, for example—needed to fulfill the command. The DBMS then determines the "least costly" method and executes the statement accordingly. Version 7.0 of ORACLE uses cost-based optimization.

daisy chain   A network topology, usually thin Ethernet, in which the network cable runs from network node to network node in a chain-like configuration.

data compression   Reduces the size of data packets for storage or transmission, using one of a number of methods. A compression algorithm shrinks the data to the smallest size possible without losing or damaging it.

data integrity (DI)   The guiding principle behind the relational model and the specific sections of the model that define how the database protects its data, and how it prevents inadvertent or unexpected modifications or damage to that data.

data-integrity rules   The SQL statements or commands in a particular RDBMS; they provide DI services.

data redundancy   The duplication of data in a database or application. It is undesirable within a single database, since it increases disk storage space and usually slows down data access. It is desirable when duplicating an entire database on a different device for backup and database integrity purposes. This second type of data redundancy is also known as *fault tolerance*.

database   A computerized collection of pieces of information, usually related to each other by some user-defined criteria.

database administrator (DBA)   The technical-support person responsible for assigning user IDs and data access permissions, creating new databases, removing databases no longer in use, and monitoring the database's disk storage usage and performance.

database application   A computer program designed to provide user access to the data in a DBMS, through data entry forms, query forms, and reports.

database dictionary   A specific type of system table that stores information about the structure of a particular database. It is primarily used in relational DBMSs to store the names and data types of the tables and columns in a database.

database engine   The portion of a DBMS that stores and manipulates the data according to commands issued from a database application.

database integrity   The theory of protecting and preserving data in a database through hardware methods, software methods, or both. Database integrity may be implemented by the DBMS itself, or through administrator intervention, such as tape backups.

database management system (DBMS)   A computer application designed for the specific purpose of collecting and storing data. It always includes a database engine and may include an application programming language or interface for creating applications.

database objects   A generic term that ORACLE, version 6.0, uses for the tables, views, and users in a database. In version 7.0, database objects include tables, views, users, snapshots, roles, profiles, procedures, packages, triggers, and integrity constraints.

database server   A computer in a client/server system that primarily runs the DBMS and processes user queries.

declarative referential integrity   The most advanced type of referential integrity. The rules for handling deletions are declared in the table definition, instead of being implemented by the application programmer through stored or precompiled SQL procedures.

disk duplexing   A method of providing database integrity whereby the application or platform automatically and simultaneously writes the data to two different disks on the same controller. If the primary disk fails, the system automatically switches to the duplexed disk and continues operating. Duplexing provides no protection against failure of the controller card.

disk mirroring   A method of providing database integrity whereby the application or platform automatically and simultaneously writes the data to two different disks on two different controllers. If one disk or card fails, the system automatically switches to the mirror disk and card and continues operating.

distributed database   A database that resides on two or more servers, yet appears to users as a single large database.

distributed database communications   The means by which two or more databases pass queries or data between themselves.

distributed database dictionary   A database dictionary that is stored on two or more database servers and is automatically updated when any changes are made to any of the databases associated with it.

distributed processing   A method of sharing application processing between two or more computer systems. Client/server databases are one of the basic forms of distributed processing.

distributed query optimization   A method of SQL command optimization designed to speed queries on distributed databases.

distributed transactions   Database transactions that are split between two or more databases in a distributed system. All portions of the transaction must be successfully completed before the whole transaction can be considered successful.

domain (data domain)   The permitted range or set of values of a particular data item in a particular field or column. For example, the domain of a column of last names could be "Words containing the characters A to Z in upper- and lowercase."

domain integrity   A principle of the relational model. It governs how the DBMS ensures that each value in a column fits in the domain of the column.

downsizing   A computer industry buzzword that describes the process of moving applications from large systems (usually mainframes) to smaller, less expensive systems (usually PCs or superservers).

encrypted file storage   A method of coding a file to prevent access by those who don't have the proper password or decoding "key."

Extended Industry Standard Architecture (EISA)   A 32-bit data bus developed as an enhancement to the ISA bus and an alternative to the MCA bus. The EISA bus is backward-compatible with ISA cards.

entity integrity   A term used by some DBMS vendors to refer to domain integrity.

expert system   An application designed to assist the user's decision making process. Expert systems are sometimes referred to as *decision support systems*.

fiber-optic cable   Networking cable that consists of one or more clear fiber threads bundled inside a protective insulator. Fiber-optic cables use intense light or lasers instead of electrical currents to transmit a signal. Fiber-optic cables suffer from less signal-strength loss than do electrical cables and are generally immune to outside interference. They also provide higher bandwidth and data transfer rates than copper cables.

field   One specific piece of information or item in a database, such as a part number or date of birth; it is referred to as a column of a single record in the relational model.

file server   A computer (usually a PC) that provides the primary shared resources on a LAN and that can be used by all the workstations or nodes on the LAN. Shared resources usually include hard-disk space and printers.

forms-based development tool   An application development tool that lets the programmer develop user-interface screens by painting a data entry form on the screen.

fourth-generation language (4GL)   An advanced computer programming language designed for creating a particular type of application, such as a database application. Examples of 4GLs include SQL and the dBASE-compatible programming languages.

front-end application   An application that runs on a client system and is designed primarily to serve as an interface between a database user and the database itself.

front-end processor (FEP)   A hardware system that handles communications with nonstandard devices, usually for a mainframe. The FEP is primarily used for dial-in access through modems and LAN attachments.

gateway system   A hardware and software system used to link two or more networks that use different protocols. Gateways are usually used to link PC-based LANs to a mainframe. A database gateway links two or more databases from different vendors together. The gateway handles all necessary SQL and data type translations.

graphical user interface (GUI)   A term used to define a class of operating systems or operating environments that base their user interfaces on graphics instead of text. Examples include Microsoft Windows 3.1, OS/2 2.0's Workplace Shell, and the Apple Macintosh's interface.

hard-disk subsystem The combination of one or more hard disks and the controller card that connects them to the rest of the computer.

hashed-clustered index Hashing creates a smaller index by substituting binary values for common elements in the index. A hashed-clustered index combines a hashed index with clustered data.

host Another term for a central computer system, such as a minicomputer or mainframe, that runs all the user and database applications. Users generally communicate with the host through terminals.

index A method used to speed access to individual data items by creating a separate construct that contains information on one or more fields in the database, sorted in a user-defined order. The index is searched, and a pointer leads the DBMS or application to the particular record the index refers to.

index file Some DBMSs store the index as a separate file on the disk, instead of storing it as part of the file that holds the database's records.

index pointer A programming construct that's included in the index file. It is used by the DBMS to find the particular data record on the disk that the indexed item refers to.

Industry Standard Architecture (ISA) A term used to describe the data bus pioneered by IBM in its PC-AT systems, that has since become the standard 16-bit bus in the industry.

integrated database API (IDAPI) Borland International's proposed database-access API. The application talks to the IDAPI driver, which handles the appropriate translations to and from the native format used by the database engine or server.

interface card Hardware that plugs into a PC's bus and connects the CPU to peripheral devices. Examples include the disk interface card (commonly called the disk controller) for connecting the CPU to the hard disks, and a parallel-interface card for connecting the PC to a printer.

interprocess communications Data communications among different processes running on the same computer system. A process can be a user application, a system function, or even different functions within the same application.

just-in-time (JIT) manufacturing   A method of reducing inventory overhead by ordering parts and assembling products as orders are received. The JIT method is sometimes modified to use a projection of expected orders over a defined period in addition to received orders.

leaf   In the hierarchical model, a leaf is the very last data node on the lowest level of a database tree.

legacy system   A common DBMS industry term for the existing PC- and host-based databases in an organization. Usually used to refer to single-user systems, or multi-user terminal-based systems.

library   A collection of programming routines that can be included in custom-written applications to provide specific functions, or speed the process of application development.

local area network (LAN)   A combination of hardware (such as interface cards and cabling) and software that lets two or more computers (usually PCs) communicate with each other to share resources.

Management Information Systems (MIS)   The usual name of the corporate department in charge of supporting computer resources. It is sometimes shortened to Information Systems (IS).

Micro Channel architecture (MCA)   A 32-bit data bus invented by IBM for its third-generation microcomputers (the PS/2 series). MCA was developed as an enhancement to and replacement for the ISA bus, and it is not backward-compatible with ISA cards.

motherboard   A generic term that describes the primary circuit board in a computer. The motherboard usually contains the support circuitry for the CPU, external ports, and data bus.

multiprocessing system   A computer system with two or more CPUs that share processing duties.

multitasking operating system   An operating system designed to perform multiple computer tasks, such as running different applications, at the same time. Microsoft Windows NT, OS/2, and Unix are examples.

multithreaded operating systems   A type of multitasking operating system that supports threads of execution that let applications multitask within themselves. Microsoft Windows NT and OS/2 are examples.

multiuser operating system   An operating system designed for running applications accessed by multiple users simultaneously through terminals and usually run on minicomputers and mainframes. IBM's MVS, Unix, and VAX/VMS are examples.

NetWare loadable module (NLM)   A program or application that executes on the file server under Novell's NetWare 3.11 or a later version of NetWare.

network administrator   The technical-support person responsible for assigning network user IDs, monitoring hard-disk space and network traffic, and ensuring that network backups are performed properly.

network interface card (NIC)   An interface card that attaches a PC to a LAN through the PC's bus. Software drivers that tell the PC how to "talk" to the card and the network are usually provided with the card or with the network software.

network topology   The cabling scheme used for a computer network, consisting of the type of cables and the way the cables are interconnected. Ethernet and Token-Ring are two examples.

network traffic   The amount of data that passes through a network during an arbitrary amount of time. The traffic indicates the network's workload versus its capacity.

node   In the hierarchical and network models, another term for a particular data item or field. Node is also used in networking to describe a single computer on the network.

non–co-located objects   An ORACLE, version 7.0, term describing database objects that reside in different databases (usually two or more distributed databases).

normalization   Used in the relational model to describe the process of designing a database's structure to reduce the amount of duplicated data. The current theory defines four levels of normalization.

off-the-shelf software   A generic term used to describe any commercial software package that can be purchased in a software store or by mail order. This type of software is not custom-written for a single company or industry.

one-to-many relationship   A database-theory term for a single data item that relates to many other items. For example, a department supervisor has a one-to-many relationship with the employees in the department.

one-to-one relationship   A database-theory term for a data item that relates to one other data item only. For example, there's a one-to-one relationship between an employee's name and Social Security number.

open database connectivity (ODBC)   Microsoft's common database-access API. The application talks to the ODBC driver, which handles the appropriate translations to and from the native format used by the database engine or server.

open system   Refers to an operating system that will run on any class of computer hardware, regardless of the vendor. MS-DOS, OS/2, PC-DOS, and Unix are examples.

package   A special type of stored procedure in version 7.0 of ORACLE that consists of one or more procedures, functions, constants, or variables. A package can be called as a unit instead of having to call each component individually.

parallel-processing system   An advanced form of multiprocessing in which a task is divided among different CPUs for processing. Each CPU handles a portion of the computations, and the final result is derived by combining all the separate calculations.

parent-child relationship   A database term that defines how two pieces of data relate to or are dependent on each other in a particular database. A child record contains data that's also contained in the parent record.

platform   A general term that refers to the hardware/software combination a particular application runs on. Specifically, the platform consists of the computer hardware and operating system.

plug-compatible   A term used to describe third-party hardware systems that are compatible with IBM mainframes. They are plug-compatible because they use the same input/output plugs as IBM hardware.

point-of-sale (POS) system   A computer application designed to supplement or replace standalone cash registers in a retail store.

population   A term that describes the specific group of information contained in the database. For example, the population of an employee database is "All the people who work for the company."

POSIX   A U.S. Federal Government standard for computer operating systems sharing the same API. POSIX allows programmers to write one application that can then be compiled and run on any POSIX-compliant system.

precompiled procedure   A SQL procedure that's compiled and stored on the same computer system as the DBMS and can be used by any application accessing the database. Unlike a stored procedure, it's not part of a particular database. Precompiled procedures are executed on the client system instead of the server.

preoptimized procedure   A precompiled or stored procedure that's optimized prior to use. Preoptimization saves CPU time and improves DBMS performance by eliminating the need to optimize a statement each time it's executed by a client application.

program analyst   A senior applications programmer who determines the end-user's application needs and designs the program to fill those needs. The analyst then gives the design to the application programmers for development.

proprietary operating systems   Computer operating systems designed to run only on a specific vendor's hardware. Digital Equipment Corp.'s VAX/VMS is an example.

record   A record is comprised of all the fields containing information about a particular individual item in a database. It is referred to as a row in the relational model.

reduced instruction-set computing (RISC)   Performed by a type of high-speed CPU that reduces the number of internal instructions it must process to carry out a computation. RISC CPUs are usually found in Unix-based workstations and superservers.

referential integrity (RI)   One of the major principles of the relational model. It is the part of data integrity that specifies how the DBMS should respond to a user's attempt to delete a parent row (record) in one table that has dependent (child) rows in another table. A proper implementation of RI ensures that child rows are never orphaned.

referential-integrity rules   The SQL statements or commands in a particular RDBMS that provide RI services.

report writer   An application or application development tool primarily designed to assist the user or programmer in creating reports from a database. Report writers usually let the user or programmer create the report layout by painting it on the screen.

request-for-proposal (RFP)   A document that describes an organization's hardware and/or software application needs. The organization sends the RFP to potential vendors, who then send a response describing how their product fits those needs.

roles   The name that version 7.0 of ORACLE uses for user groups. Users can be designated as part of a role, and security rights can be granted on a role basis.

router   A hardware/software combination that joins two or more LANs. A router can link LANs using different topologies and protocols. Routers also reduce network traffic by passing only the data destined for the interconnected LAN(s) while filtering out data that should remain on the source LAN.

scalability   The characteristic of applications or databases that run on multiple platforms of varying sizes. For example, an ORACLE database can run on a PC or a VAX. Computers can also be scalable by having the ability to add more CPUs in the same physical system.

scrollable cursor   A SQL construct that lets the user browse forward and backward through all the data returned in response to a query, instead of receiving and viewing the results one row at a time, in the forward direction.

server process   ORACLE, version 7.0's term for a task started by the RDBMS to handle one or more user requests.

session   A logical connection between a user and a database in version 7.0 of ORACLE. Every user can have more than one session established to more than one database, depending on the configuration of the databases involved.

shared SQL areas   A common memory buffer in version 7.0 of ORACLE used to store compiled SQL statements that can be executed by any user application. A stored procedure is created outside of any application and

stored with the database; in contrast, a shared SQL statement is dynamically loaded into the memory buffer the first time an application uses it.

sibling relationship   The characteristic of two or more pieces of information that are related to one another and are equal in importance. It's another way of describing the fields in a record; for example, the name, address, and phone number of an employee are each in sibling relationships with one another and with any data describing that employee.

small computer system interface (SCSI)   A standard method for connecting data peripherals to a microcomputer, usually used for storage devices such as disks, tape drives, and CD-ROM drives.

star configuration   A type of network topology in which the cables that connect the nodes to the network emanate from a central hub, with one cable per node. It is sometimes referred to as a hub-and-star configuration.

stored procedures   SQL procedures that are stored as part of the transaction logic of a database and executed entirely on the back-end system. Stored procedures let you move more of the database processing from the client to the server.

supercomputers   High-speed, high-powered computers predominantly used for intense scientific calculations, such as weather predictions and engineering design.

symmetrical multiprocessing (SMP)   A multiprocessing system in which processing tasks are divided between various CPUs. Each new task is routed to the CPU with the lowest workload at the time of processing.

syntax-based optimization   The original method of optimizing SQL statements, whereby the DBMS analyzes the commands for the most logical order of executing them, without regard to the CPU time and resources needed. Syntax-based optimizers are generally slower and more resource-intensive than cost-based optimizers. Version 6.0 of ORACLE uses a variation of syntax-based optimization, called rule-based optimization.

system tables   A special database used by some DBMSs to store information about the whole database system; for example, it identifies individual databases contained in the system, and user security access information. Primarily used in DBMSs that follow the relational model.

terminal controller   A hardware subsystem that handles the communications between terminals and the central host. Usually used with minicomputers and mainframes, it can connect up to 64 terminals to the host through a single host connection.

terminal, dumb   A dedicated system connected to a central host that generally consists of only a display screen and keyboard. It sends keystrokes to the host and displays the screen information sent back from the host.

terminal, intelligent   A type of terminal connected to a central computer host that has its own CPU for handling some of the processing, such as screen drawing and network communications; it may or may not be a dedicated system. A PC is an example of an intelligent terminal when it's connected via a specialized peripheral board to a mainframe.

third-generation language (3GL)   A general-purpose computer programming language used to create any type of application. Examples of 3GLs include BASIC, C, COBOL, and Pascal.

third-party add-on   A hardware or software product developed by one vendor to work with and enhance another vendor's product.

thread   A process within an application that carries out a particular operation or task. Single-threaded applications can do only one task at a time. Multithreaded applications can do multiple tasks simultaneously, such as sorting a database while printing a report. The ability to perform multiple threads within an application is usually provided by the operating system.

transaction recovery logs   Log files maintained by a DBMS that keep a record of every recent transaction performed on a database. They provide data integrity services by giving the DBMS a means of returning the database to a consistent state if a transaction fails or the system crashes. These files are usually referred to as simply the transaction logs.

transmission control protocol/internet protocol (TCP/IP)   A networking protocol that originated in the U.S. Department of Defense for linking their Unix systems with other computers. It is now the most common inter-platform networking protocol for systems ranging from PCs to mainframes.

trigger   A particular type of stored procedure that is automatically executed when certain SQL commands (usually those that modify the data) are issued. Called *rules* by some vendors, triggers usually implement RI in systems that don't support declarative RI.

twisted-pair cable Electrical network cable consisting of two or more pieces of insulated wire twisted together and covered with one or more insulation layers. Round telephone wire is a familiar example.

two-phase commit A form of transaction processing on multiple databases (or multiple tables within a database) that ensures that modifications made to every database involved in a transaction are successful before the transaction itself is considered successful.

upsizing Moving an application from a smaller system to a larger one as the need for disk storage space and processing power grows. It usually refers to moving a PC-based database to a Unix-based superserver.

user-transparent A characteristic of systems in which data processing actions are taken without the user being aware of them or manually performing them. For example, a user sends a query to a local database server, and the server automatically passes the query to another server where the data actually resides.

value-added reseller (VAR) A type of computer system consultant that provides complete application solutions, including all the necessary software. VARs sometimes provide the hardware needed to run the application as well.

vertical market application A specialized application designed for a particular business or organizational function. Vertical market applications are usually written and sold by VARs.

virtual memory (VM) A method whereby an operating system swaps inactive data and code to available disk space, freeing up working RAM for active applications. The data and code is swapped to the disk in *pages* (the size of the page is dependent on the CPU), so the process is sometimes referred to as virtual-memory paging or simply paging. OS/2 and Unix are examples of operating systems that use virtual memory.

wide-area network (WAN) A network that connects computer systems that span more than one building. A WAN generally consists of one or more LANs in separate locations that are interconnected directly or through a central host.

INDEX

Ziff-Davis Press Survey of Readers

Please help us in our effort to produce the best books on personal computing.
For your assistance, we would be pleased to send you a FREE catalog
featuring the complete line of Ziff-Davis Press books.

1. How did you first learn about this book?

Recommended by a friend . . . . ☐ -1 (5)

Recommended by store personnel . . . . ☐ -2

Saw in Ziff-Davis Press catalog . . . . ☐ -3

Received advertisement in the mail . . . . ☐ -4

Saw the book on bookshelf at store . . . . ☐ -5

Read book review in: _____ ☐ -6

Saw an advertisement in: _____ ☐ -7

Other (Please specify): _____ ☐ -8

2. Which THREE of the following factors most influenced your decision to purchase this book? (Please check up to THREE.)

Front or back cover information on book . . . ☐ -1 (6)

Logo of magazine affiliated with book . . . . . . ☐ -2

Special approach to the content . . . . ☐ -3

Completeness of content . . . . ☐ -4

Author's reputation. . . . . ☐ -5

Publisher's reputation . . . . ☐ -6

Book cover design or layout . . . . ☐ -7

Index or table of contents of book . . . . ☐ -8

Price of book . . . . ☐ -9

Special effects, graphics, illustrations . . . . . . ☐ -0

Other (Please specify): _____ ☐ -x

3. How many computer books have you purchased in the last six months? _____ (7-10)

4. On a scale of 1 to 5, where 5 is excellent, 4 is above average, 3 is average, 2 is below average, and 1 is poor, please rate each of the following aspects of this book below. (Please circle your answer.)

Depth/completeness of coverage	5	4	3	2	1	(11)
Organization of material	5	4	3	2	1	(12)
Ease of finding topic	5	4	3	2	1	(13)
Special features/time saving tips	5	4	3	2	1	(14)
Appropriate level of writing	5	4	3	2	1	(15)
Usefulness of table of contents	5	4	3	2	1	(16)
Usefulness of index	5	4	3	2	1	(17)
Usefulness of accompanying disk	5	4	3	2	1	(18)
Usefulness of illustrations/graphics	5	4	3	2	1	(19)
Cover design and attractiveness	5	4	3	2	1	(20)
Overall design and layout of book	5	4	3	2	1	(21)
Overall satisfaction with book	5	4	3	2	1	(22)

5. Which of the following computer publications do you read regularly; that is, 3 out of 4 issues?

Byte . . . . ☐ -1 (23)

Computer Shopper . . . . ☐ -2

Corporate Computing . . . . ☐ -3

Dr. Dobb's Journal . . . . ☐ -4

LAN Magazine . . . . ☐ -5

MacWEEK . . . . ☐ -6

MacUser . . . . ☐ -7

PC Computing . . . . ☐ -8

PC Magazine . . . . ☐ -9

PC WEEK . . . . ☐ -0

Windows Sources . . . . ☐ -x

Other (Please specify): _____ ☐ -y

Please turn page.

6. What is your level of experience with personal computers? With the subject of this book?

	With PCs	With subject of book
Beginner.............	☐ -1 (24)	☐ -1 (25)
Intermediate..........	☐ -2	☐ -2
Advanced.............	☐ -3	☐ -3

7. Which of the following best describes your job title?

Officer (CEO/President/VP/owner)........	☐ -1 (26)
Director/head.....................	☐ -2
Manager/supervisor....................	☐ -3
Administration/staff....................	☐ -4
Teacher/educator/trainer.................	☐ -5
Lawyer/doctor/medical professional........	☐ -6
Engineer/technician....................	☐ -7
Consultant..........................	☐ -8
Not employed/student/retired.............	☐ -9
Other (Please specify): _____	☐ -0

8. What is your age?

Under 20............................	☐ -1 (27)
21-29..............................	☐ -2
30-39..............................	☐ -3
40-49..............................	☐ -4
50-59..............................	☐ -5
60 or over..........................	☐ -6

9. Are you:

Male...............................	☐ -1 (28)
Female.............................	☐ -2

Thank you for your assistance with this important information! Please write your address below to receive our free catalog.

Name: _____

Address: _____

City/State/Zip: _____

Fold here to mail.

1218-04-04

_____

_____

_____